Eating the Wedding Gifts

Eating *the* Wedding Gifts

LEAN YEARS AFTER MARRIAGE BREAK-UP

J. GORDON SHILLINGFORD
PUBLISHING INC

Cover and interior design by Relish Design Studio Ltd.

We acknowledge the financial support of the Manitoba Arts Council, The Canada Council for the Arts and the Government of Canada through the Book Publishing Industry Development Program (BPIDP) for our publishing program.

Printed and bound in Canada

Library and Archives Canada Cataloguing in Publication

Murphy, Barbara
    Eating the wedding gifts : Lean years after marriage break-up / Barbara Murphy.

Includes bibliographical references and index.
ISBN 0-920486-90-8

    1. Divorced women–Education–Canada. 2. Divorced women–Canada–Economic conditions. 3. Women–Education (Higher)–Canada. I. Title.

LC1767.M87 2005   305.48'96942'0971   C2005-903967-1

J. Gordon Shillingford Publishing Inc.
P.O. Box 86, RPO Corydon Avenue, Winnipeg, MB R3M 3S3

Acknowledgements

I am greatly indebted to the many single parents who volunteered to share their stories for this project. I have used fictitious names to maintain confidentiality and, in some cases, have changed other details of their lives that might identify them. Their stories tell of challenges they faced, both financial and emotional – challenges that would defeat most of us. In a real sense they are heroines, and their children can be proud of them.

Kathy Secord and Colleen Hendrick gave advice and encouragement when the project was still taking shape in my mind. Johanne Tallon, Colleen Hendrick, and Danielle Massé of the City of Ottawa helped get the word out that I was looking for volunteers. I am grateful to all of them for making this possible.

Table of Contents

Chapter 1

RECENT TRENDS AFFECTING WOMEN

If asked about her hopes and dreams for the future, not a single teenaged girl will answer: "I've always wanted to live in poverty." Yet many make choices that bring about that unhappy ending. And still others simply drift into it without making choices at all.

As their final years of high school approach, Canadian students make decisions at least for the short term, if not for the long. For generations past, parents have felt an obligation to discuss the future with their sons—they have listened, offered advice, and encouraged. Some parents, but fewer, even discussed career plans with their daughters. Today, parent expectations are still an important variable in the career decisions of high school graduates as many research interview studies have revealed. The most notable change has been that serious planning has increasingly included female students who are now urged to plan for a lifetime of financial independence just as male students do.

Sadly, the transition is not yet complete. Many female high school students are still left without appropriate parental advice. And perhaps they are not yet seriously helped by guidance counsellors either. Wherever the gap, it translates into thousands of young Canadian women choosing to follow high school with dead-end employment and, in short order, marriage.

Some harsh realities face these young women. Today almost 40 percent of Canadian marriages will end in divorce, and the rate is higher for earlier marriages. The peak year for divorce is the fifth year of marriage; many early brides, therefore, will become single parents before they are 25 years of age. But marriage breakdown is only the first of the misfortunes they will suffer. According to the National Council of Welfare, over 93 percent of single parents under 25 live below the poverty line.[1] They are five times more likely to be poor than the average Canadian, and the reasons for their poverty are not difficult to find. Almost 50 percent of women with young children will not hold jobs after their divorce because they will have more than one child to care for (1.6 to be exact). Without work, they will be on welfare with allowance levels all across the country so far below the poverty line they are out of sight. Even those who manage to find child care and a job are likely to experience financial hardship. The large majority of single parents who work will be restricted by their high school diplomas to the lowest paid jobs in Canada.

Fair or not, those are the two most likely sources of income to pay the rent and put food on the table. A whopping 83 percent of single parents will not receive child support from their ex-husbands[2] (in Ontario alone, somewhere in the neighbourhood of 90,000 support orders went unpaid in the 1990s[3]). And this despite the fact that after divorce, while the incomes of divorced wives drop dramatically, the incomes of their ex-husbands increase.

If these are depressing facts and figures, some separated or divorced women with children have managed to escape poverty. A small percentage of single parents have a university degree (8 percent[4]) which means that at least 8 percent have incomes well above the poverty line, some in the top category of Canadian incomes. Why they have been the lucky ones is not a secret. In every province in Canada, and in every year in both this century and the last, Canadians with university degrees earned more than those with high school education, as much as $22,000 more annually in the year 2000[5]. The earnings advantage is as true for women as it is for men.

Over the past 20 years the number of women who have completed university in Canada has tripled, until today more Canadian women than men have university degrees. This is a major trend that has largely gone unnoticed by many Canadians. No government policy or program can claim credit; it simply reflects the conscious decisions of many women to prepare themselves for a lifetime of work at an income that will provide independence. Just as important, it reflects the beginning of the end of the traditional neglect of our daughters when they come to make decisions about their future.

Fifty years ago, when the grandmothers of today's high school seniors were young, women rarely questioned the universally held truth that they would depend solely on a male breadwinner for most of their adult lives. Even as recently as 30 years ago women were expected to move on to marriage soon after high school. While the expectations for male high school students were more likely to include university, sights were set lower for women. One study of Ontario high school students in the 1970s found that, especially among lower-income students, 42 percent of girls expected to go to work following high school, rather than go on to university, compared to 18 percent of boys.[6] Interviews with parents revealed they were more willing to make difficult financial sacrifices for the higher education of their sons than for the higher education of their daughters. These decisions reflected the still common belief that university education would be wasted on young women whose more important goal should be to find a husband to look after them.

In the intervening years, however, much has changed. Today female high school students have other options, all of them taking for granted a lifelong goal of financial independence. Over the next ten years they can become dentists, geologists, school principals, lawyers, professors, doctors, senior managers, or judges, to name only a few of the highest paid occupations in Canada.

With all these options open, what has happened to promising young women after high school that finds so many of them living in poverty with young children? The answer lies in those fateful decisions made at graduation; too many young women have settled for undemanding jobs and early marriage. The order may even have been reversed. Did parents and counsellors fail to tell them they were cut out for more? Young men and women make their own decisions at this critical juncture in their lives, but there remains an important role in laying out the costs and benefits of the roads to be taken.

Among all options, early marriage has proven to be the most precarious. International studies have shown that, even though there are differences between male and female marrying ages (with men still a few years older), both educated men and women marry late while the less educated marry at an early age.[7] In addition, women across the world are increasingly marrying later, getting closer to the marrying age of men, a trend that reflects that young women are now more likely to prepare for life, rather than simply for marriage and motherhood.

—•—

Two demographic trends affecting Canadian women have grown alongside each other over the past 30 years. One has been positive for women—women university graduates now make up the larger part of all university graduates. The other has been negative—single-parent families living in poverty are a growing share of all families. These developments have occurred quite independently, as if the lucky and the unlucky were not aware of the others' existence. All of these women, however, live in the same country, in the same cities, and at one time they went to the same high schools. Though they shared the same world at high school a few short years ago, sadly they are in different worlds now. Most of us can readily choose which world we prefer for our daughters.

EATING THE WEDDING GIFTS

Of these two late 20th-century trends, the increase in single-parent families is the bad news. It has been 30 years in the making. The trend away from the two-parent family as the social norm in Canada began in the 1970s after three-quarters of a century during which single-parent families had actually declined from a peak in the latter years of the Victorian era.

Although the Victorian years seem an unlikely period for single-parent families to peak in number, a history of families in Canada reveals that a hundred years ago the death of a young or middle-aged husband was not rare. War, industrial accidents, and high death rates from infectious diseases took their toll on men long before old age, leaving widows with the care of children and few financial resources. Widowhood was, in fact, the major reason women were left on their own with children. Widows made up the vast majority of single parents while today they represent less than a fifth.[8] Their plight was not unlike the plight of present-day single parents: most lived in poverty.

As the century progressed, however, the cause of marriage breakdown shifted from death to divorce, as a long struggle to overturn public attitudes took place. A number of social historians have examined the changes to divorce practices through the years, changes that were always in the direction of easier divorce. They have put in context today's high divorce rates and society's almost total acceptance.

In *Putting Asunder*, the most recent of these social histories, Roderick Phillips describes the barriers to divorce from the Middle Ages up to the mid-19th century and the gradual easing of those barriers from that time until the present.[9] Early restrictions on divorce reflected the sanctity of marriage in church doctrine in most Western countries and the strong influence of the church on the laws and institutions of society. Even by the end of the 19th century very few marriages worldwide were ending in divorce. At that time in Canada there were only 12 legal divorces a year on average across the country.

barbara murphy

The fact that divorce did not easily shake off an image as a moral and social evil can be found in the very nature of legislation for almost a hundred years after it was first introduced. In divorce applications the legal machinery involved one partner in a marriage accusing the other of wrongdoing. Since the wrongdoing in nearly all cases was adultery, a certain amount of stigma was attached to divorce. Divorce was widely recognized as a failure on the part of both spouses, not only the partner guilty of the offense.

There were other reasons for the low rate of divorce besides the scandal attached to marriage breakdown. One of the most important was the high cost, which put divorce proceedings beyond the reach of everyone but the upper classes. In England and countries of the British Empire divorce could only be granted by individual Act of Parliament, a cumbersome, long, and expensive process.

In addition, a whole range of other barriers in 19th-century society made it inconceivable for most men and women to dissolve their marriage no matter how impossible it had become or how many new laws were passed to allow one of the partners to end it. For one thing, husbands and wives depended on each other economically to a far greater extent than they do today. Although a new industrial economy had almost replaced the old type of family economy, in which every member of the family worked in the home in a shared economic enterprise, there was still a large rural population by the late 19th century where exactly that type of family economy prevailed. In predominantly rural Canada an unhappy husband needed his wife for economic reasons as much as she needed him.

Besides these realities, and for women especially, there were few practical alternatives for living outside of marriage. In considering divorce, a wife knew she could take nothing with her since property legally belonged to the breadwinner husband. Instead she could look forward to living in extreme poverty with her children unless she could move back in with parents or could qualify for some form of charity. Either solution, however, was not a certainty, especially a reliance on charity, which was often extended to widows but rarely to women who voluntarily left their husbands.

These very real deterrents to dissolving a marriage effectively locked spouses together when either one might wish otherwise. As a result, they often adapted themselves to difficult situations and put up with negative behaviour in marriage that would not be tolerated today. In his history of divorce, Phillips writes of the 19th century:

> ... marriages lasted not necessarily because the spouses were morally superior to later cohorts of husbands and wives, nor because they loved each other more deeply or cared more for their children, nor because they worked harder at their marriages and were less fickle than their descendants, but simply because there was nothing else they could do, and they accommodated to that reality.[10]

While these economic and practical considerations kept divorce rates low, change was on the way. As society became more urban in the 20th century, new work patterns came to the fore. Individuals were more likely to earn individual wages rather than contributing to a family economy and, in doing so, they gained an increasing amount of independence. These changes weakened the economic ties that had locked spouses into marriage, especially as women began to find employment outside the home, opening up possibilities of escape for those who wanted out.

At the same time attitudes about divorce began to change. Religious ties were weakening in most Western societies and the holiness of holy matrimony was less vigorously upheld by the general public. It was inevitable that more tolerant attitudes accompanied this trend—in fact, there are good arguments that more tolerant attitudes came first and the weakening of religious ties afterward. As divorce began to lose much of its scandalous reputation, it became more acceptable to bring unsatisfactory marriages to an end, short of murder. The rate of public acceptance slowly climbed through the

barbara murphy

century—while only a quarter of Canadians in 1943 favoured easier divorces, by 1960 over half were in favour.[11]

Changes in legislation followed, but slowly. The average of 12 legal divorces a year in Canada at the turn of the century became 26 a year in the first decade of the 20th and then edged up to 54 a year in the period leading up to World War I.[12] These were not large numbers, but divorces in most provinces of Canada were still being granted only through private Acts of Parliament. As legal approvals for divorce were finally transferred to provincial civil courts, the number of divorces increased, although adultery was still the only grounds. Canada lagged behind many other countries for years in this narrow definition.

With access to provincial courts the number of divorce applications in Canada climbed from an average of less than 7,000 a year after World War II to 11,000 by the late 1960s.[13] These numbers, indicating far greater public acceptance of divorce and the need for divorce legislation to keep pace, finally brought federal action in the form of a new Divorce Act, which allowed unlimited grounds for divorce without attempting to attribute fault to one partner or the other. By 1969 Canadian couples could be granted a divorce for any reason if they were separated for at least three years.

The shift to "no-fault" divorce in Canada simply followed what was happening in most Western countries. New policies in these countries finally overthrew the old principle that the church or state should regulate divorce. Though it had taken some time, divorce policies now discarded their moralistic nature and removed the last barrier to accessibility. It had an immediate effect—the divorce rate in Canada shot up from 14 percent of all marriages in 1969 (the first year of the new legislation) to 30 percent in just six years.[14] A further surge followed in the 1980s when the required separation years for no-fault divorce were reduced to one. In 1987 the divorce rate peaked at 48 percent, or almost half of all marriages were ending in divorce.

EATING THE WEDDING GIFTS

More divorces, of course, translated into more single-parent families and a shift to divorced women, rather than widows, as family heads. Before the introduction of no-fault divorce legislation, widows still made up 60 percent of single-parent families in Canada. Today, divorced women make up the majority. Along with separated women, who sometimes fail to show up in statistics, they almost wholly account for the dramatic increase in single-parent families over the past 30 years.[15]

Years in the making, it is remarkable that these changes seem to have taken so many by surprise. It is no longer useful to leave the future of young women to chance or to trivialize their potential by preparing them only for marriage and a life of dependence. Unfortunately, it is no longer kind to keep the odds from starry-eyed brides.

In contrast, there was good news in another demographic trend affecting the lives of Canadian women in the last quarter of the 20th century. While a growing number were becoming single parents as a result of marriage breakdown, hundreds of other women were graduating from universities in Canada at an unprecedented rate. In doing so, they were shifting Canada's population of degree holders to a predominantly female population for the first time in history.

Reaching this milestone was all the more incredible in light of the century-old struggle women had fought simply to be admitted to any of the country's universities. It was 1875 before the first Canadian woman was granted a university degree despite the fact that there were over a dozen universities in existence in Canada by mid-19th century. Graduating from Mount Allison University in New Brunswick, she was not only the first woman to graduate in Canada but the first in the British Empire.[16] Over the next decade, Acadia, Queen's, Dalhousie, Toronto, and Trinity universities granted degrees to ten more women in total, and by the end of the century over

barbara murphy

a hundred women had graduated from various Canadian universities. While this represented considerable progress, women still represented only 12 percent of undergraduate students by 1900.

Fortunately there are diaries and records of these first women students and the traditional attitudes they had to over-come in the 19th century. Margaret Gillett, in her history of women at McGill, records a few of the comments made by well-known figures of that period on the subject of educating women. By now the most famous is the advice given to any aspiring female student by Charles Kingsley, author and pro-fessor of English at Cambridge: "Be good, sweet maid, and let who can be clever."[17] At Oxford women were also given short shrift. John Ruskin, art critic and professor of art at Oxford, when asked to admit women to his lecture, replied: "I cannot let the bonnets in on any condition..."[18] He was not the only one to trivialize the issue in the hope the demands of a small group of women would go away. *Punch*, the English weekly, ran the following verses in 1875:

Sally was a pretty girl
Fanny was her sister;
Sally read all night and day
Fanny sighed and kissed her.

Sally won some school degrees
Fanny won a lover;
Sally soundly rated her,
And thought herself above her.

Fanny had a happy home,
And urged that plea only;
Sally she was learned—and
Also she was lonely.[19]

EATING THE WEDDING GIFTS

In a similar tone, Canadian Stephen Leacock, humorist and professor of economics at McGill, wrote about the early female students: "At McGill the girls of our first year have wept over their failures in elementary physics these twenty-five years. It is time that someone dried their tears and took away the subject."[20]

And then there were the claims of those who were deadly serious, also quoted in Gillett's history. Best-selling author and physician Edward Clarke wrote in 1873 that women's physiology was simply not organized for the strain of brain work. On the subject of women students attending lectures with men, he claimed that co-education could be harmful, inducing neuralgia, uterine disease, and hysteria. American psychologist G. Stanley Hall warned that for women to have the same education as men ran counter to the prevailing view of motherhood. Other researchers claimed that colleges attracted the type of women who were lacking in normal sex instincts.

These public attitudes had an impact on parents' plans for their adolescents. Many refused to send their daughters to university. Despite these attitudes a number of young women doggedly pursued their educational goals each year in the face of popular resistance and derision until their acceptance as undergraduates in universities across the country became less and less controversial.

There was still considerable controversy, however, surrounding the admission of women into the traditional male professions of medicine, law, and engineering. For those who aspired to entry into those courses of study it was as if the battle had to be fought all over again. By the late 19th century, for example, only a handful of Canadian women had gained entry to medical schools.

A whole new litany of dreadful consequences was put forth by people opposed to the idea of women doctors. For one, the study of anatomy would surely cause a young woman to lose her maidenly modesty; for another, it would turn the familiar warmth of feminine emotions into something cold. It was also argued that the health of women was too uncertain

barbara murphy

for the rigours of advanced study, their endurance too limited, and their nerves too weak. Or their preoccupation with fashion would jeopardize the health of their patients. One medical professor quipped: "... can you think of a patient in a critical case [requiring surgery], waiting for half an hour while the medical lady fixes her bonnet or adjusts her bustle?"[21]

When women were finally admitted into medicine, many medical schools approved only if separate classes in dissection were held for men and women students. Some schools also imposed higher academic admission requirements for women than for men. Despite these barriers along the way, the presence of women students in Canadian medical schools became a fact of life throughout the 20th century. When women responded to some of the earlier concerns about their ability by winning their share of prizes at graduation, opponents attributed their success to the fact that they worked harder than men, and everyone was allowed to save face.

There was similar resistance to women entering the law profession in the 19th century. One academic writer argued at the time that "the severe searching mind that gives eminence to the lawyer is foreign to [women's] usual constitution."[22] By 1891, however, two women were finally enrolled in Canadian law schools (compared to 308 male students). Some provinces, however, allowed women to complete studies in law and receive a degree but refused to allow them to be members of the provincial Bar. This effectively excluded them from the practice of law, an exclusion that was justified on the grounds that pretty women lawyers might improperly sway juries. A Quebec application by a woman graduate to take the Bar examination was dismissed with the following judgment:

> ... to admit a woman, and more particularly a married woman, as a barrister—that is to say as a person who pleads cases at the Bar before judges and juries in open court and in the presence of the public, would be nothing short of a direct infringement of public order and a manifest violation of the law of good morals and public decency.[23]

EATING THE WEDDING GIFTS

In these early years admission into schools of architecture was also denied women who, it was claimed, could not physically stand long hours of draughting. Finally gaining admission to three Canadian schools of architecture, women still faced difficulties after graduation. One young woman graduate looking for her first job was told by a potential employer that she should stay home because "there is plenty of architecture around the house."[24]

As a result of these early struggles, women grew from less than 2 percent of university enrolment across the country in 1881 to 20 percent by 1911. But even more dramatic gains were made as the century progressed. By the 1960s, with changing attitudes about appropriate roles for women, more and more female students were attracted into Canadian universities. By the late 1980s more women than men were acquiring bachelor degrees and, in several Canadian universities, women began to constitute the majority of the graduating classes in faculties of law and medicine.

This was not only evidence of the educational levels women could reach, it was a reflection of the increasingly career-oriented decisions made by young women after completing high school. While earlier studies had consistently shown that, despite better academic records, female high school students were less likely to go on to university than male students, this was no longer the case.[25] Equal proportions of male and female high school students were now going on to university. More women were looking ahead to ensure their own economic independence over a lifetime than did their mothers or grandmothers.

This trend coincided with the marked trend toward later marriage and later age for the birth of a first child. It was clear more women were realizing that early marriage and motherhood were incompatible with their long-range goals of taking charge of their own lives. While their decisions required some discipline and sacrifice in the short run, most had no intention of giving up the satisfaction of marriage and motherhood forever.

Barbara Murphy

—·—

Two trends affecting Canadian women over the last 30 years have given a new look to the future we can predict for today's female high school graduates. We can be heartened by better outlooks for some and saddened by the misfortune facing others. More women are going on to higher education—they make up the largest group of women and, in choosing this path, they have a good deal of assurance of financial independence throughout their lives whether married or not. Other women choose work following high school. The only assurance they have is that the work will be low-wage work. Among these low-wage women, some will marry and live happily ever after in a one- or two-income household; some will marry and within a few years find themselves single parents living in poverty. Clearly these are not the only outcomes—some may back-pack through Europe and Asia, some may become overnight rock stars—but the majority will find themselves in one of these situations.

The choices seem straightforward, but young women make decisions about the future in the context of many other things going on in their lives at the end of high school. So while it can be argued that they make their choices based on their own personal motivations and desires, there are larger social forces they cannot always control. Both the personal and social constraints on their decisions are covered in the following chapters.

Social scientists in the field of "life course" research have identified the social (or structural) constraints that are beyond control when a young person decides about the future—the state of the economy, gender, social class, and ethnicity, among others. At the same time they contend that we should guard against focussing attention on structural forces while de-emphasizing personal choice.[26] This is a more promising approach and one I have tried to use in tracing the happy and not-so-happy futures young women can expect.

Chapter 2

INFLUENCES ON
POST-SECONDARY DECISIONS

How high school students make decisions about going directly to work or going on to university is related to many other things happening in their lives as they move from adolescence into adulthood. On a personal level they are in the process of developing their own inner standards to guide their behaviour and these have become more important motivators than the external rules that guided them in their younger years. Society roughly equates this development with maturity. Among other things, it also includes better control of impulses and greater acceptance of responsibility.

At the same time, adolescents on the threshold of becoming adults are placing a greater value on interpersonal concerns. The development of their own individuality is taking place in the midst of an ever-expanding number of connections and relationships.

When these personal changes coincide with a life stage that society considers important—the end of compulsory schooling—the future can be anything but clear for many young high school students. In making decisions, they must weigh personal factors such as their own hopes and dreams for the future, the expectations of their parents, and the plans of their friends and other peers against broader social influences like gender, social class, ethnicity, the cost of higher education, and the nature of the labour market.

The weight placed on all these factors when students decide about university has been the subject of considerable study. In light of greater enrolments of students from middle and upper class families in universities, income would appear to be important. Surprisingly, however, most research has shown that students are less influenced by financial considerations than by the expectations of their parents.[27] Indeed, the impact of parents' expectations has held true for as long as universities have been in existence. Even as they became institutions serving a broader constituency in the last half of the 20th century, the impact has been as powerful for students from low-income families as it has been for students from families with higher incomes. For example, in the case of males in an Ontario study, lower-income students whose parents had high expectations of post-secondary enrolment were almost four times more likely to enrol in post-secondary education than lower-income students whose parents had low expectations.[28] This gap in outcomes, in fact, followed the identical pattern as that for higher-income students whose parents would not face the same financial barriers to any high hopes they might hold for their offspring.

The strongest evidence that parent expectations are a more important influence on students than financial resources is found in the higher educational outcomes of high school graduates from immigrant families. The same Ontario study found that, while parent incomes were dramatically lower than the average income of Canadian-born parents, the expectations of immigrant parents for their children's post-secondary education were every bit as high, if not higher. Over 48 percent of foreign-born parents of high school graduates expected their children to attend university compared to 42 percent of Canadian-born parents.[29]

With these high expectations, students with foreign-born parents went on to high levels of university completion, surpassing the performance of students with Canadian-born parents. Roughly 40 percent of high school graduates from immigrant families completed university compared to 33 percent of those with Canadian-born parents.[30]

Successful outcomes for immigrants have been attributed by researchers to the determination of foreign-born parents to have their children achieve a higher level of occupational success than they achieved themselves. They see education as the way to career opportunities and life goals. While this is also the motivation of Canadian-born parents, foreign-born parents and their children must find ways around the barriers to achievement that can be put up by a sometimes unfriendly and discriminating society. Immigrant families use education to help deal with these barriers because it allows them to achieve and succeed on merit.

The link between education and employment has been clear to immigrant families. Besides their educational over-achievement, first-generation Canadians show a remarkable degree of upward occupational mobility. After university graduation they occupy managerial, science and engineering, and medical occupations out of proportion to their numbers, and their occupational levels tend to get higher over the life of their careers. In fact, researchers have found, children of foreign-born parents may begin with a socio-economic status disadvantage but they end up twenty years later better off than their peers with Canadian-born parents.

While immigrant parents may outclass Canadian-born parents in the high expectations department, both kinds of parents have been less than even-handed in their expectations for their sons and daughters. Historically, daughters have not rated as high in parent expectations as sons but, like all findings related to women in the past two decades, things are changing. A 1971 study of Canadian high school students found that, especially in the case of girls from low-income families, parent expectations were not as high for girls as for boys, a finding that researchers attributed to a lower value placed by parents on an extended education for

barbara murphy

their daughters.[31] A study of Ontario high school students came up with similar findings, showing greater interest and encouragement from lower-income parents in their sons' education than for their daughters and less willingness to support their daughters financially.[32]

By the 1980s a study of Hamilton, Halifax, and rural Nova Scotia students revealed a shift in this historical pattern. More parents preferred and expected their daughters than their sons to attend university.[33] As we have seen, this shift has been reflected in the increasing enrolment of women in university since the 1970s to the point where it now exceeds the enrolment of men.

What parents do to make their expectations known in a subtle and often not-so-subtle fashion has been reported by students interviewed in these Canadian studies. A sample of comments from those who enrolled in university is typical. One Toronto student stated that there was never any decision to be made as to whether he would go on to university. Rather it was more a question of *when* he would go.[34] A student raised in rural Ontario recalled: "... my father said to me when I was young ... I'd like to see you better than me." A female student reported a conversation with her father in which he strongly advised further education: "He told me I had to think of the future, that if I didn't marry I would have to support myself."[35] Another remembered her mother's support: "She always encouraged us to have a career so we wouldn't be dependent upon a man." And still another: "You know how parents are ... It was like brainwashing."

On the flip side of the coin, parents could also affect the decision-making of their adolescents by actively discouraging higher education or taking a neutral stance. The comments of those who did not go on to university show how the message got through. One student recalled: "Nothing was ever discussed. I just got out of high school and worked." And another, interpreting her mother's lack of encouragement: "She thinks a woman doesn't have a need for further education." Another was just as clear about her father's message: "He discouraged me because he was old-fashioned in that [he thought] women don't need education."

That parent expectations have the most significant influence of all influences on young people's educational decisions takes on additional meaning when students are also asked about others who were important to their choices. In the study of Hamilton, Halifax, and rural Nova Scotia students, parents were identified as most important 5 to 10 times more often than teachers, counsellors, or peers (mothers 10 times more often and fathers 5 times more often).[36] On a more positive note, although other individuals in students' lives were not ranked *most* important, about a quarter of students ranked teachers and guidance counsellors as *very* important. Admittedly this is not a proportion to cause celebration, but it is clear these could become strong influences, especially for students whose parents are not playing a significant role.

— • —

For all income groups, then, and for both genders, parent expectations play a significant role in decisions about university. With this new moral support women have now caught up to men in university enrolment and graduation. Their parents' wishes have been strong motivators, but the women who have brought about this important gain have made their own personal decisions. The benefits of educational equality to Canadian society at large have really been the outcome of many individual actions.

Despite these giant steps, however, there are still many Canadian women without university or college completion, with results that are far more calamitous than they are for males. Instead they have gone to work following high school for a number of reasons, and have married without higher education credentials in their resumés. Their chances of realizing the potential they showed in high school are poor, as statistics on marriage breakdown and female wage scales have shown.

barbara murphy

Given the obvious advantage to university graduates of higher lifetime incomes, why are so many women not making this choice? To understand their decisions, it can be useful to look at some of the influences pulling them in other directions, influences that may apply to both male and female students but are considered here as they apply to female students who have somehow stayed apart from the dramatic shift toward the predominance of women in Canadian universities.

For many female students in the last years of high school, a growing impatience with the routine of twelve long years of schooling can affect their decisions about going on to further education. They have had their fill of class work, homework, and what seems at times to be "make-work." They question the relevance of class material to what they will need in the real world outside school, and they fear that higher education will be more of the same.

Confirming this, almost half of students not choosing university report that they find schoolwork boring and that this fact influenced their decision.[37] This has been as true for female students as for males. In a sense they have lost enthusiasm with learning, with being "taught at"—a passive role that seems a poor substitute for spreading their wings. Moreover, the pressure of maintaining good grades on assignments and exams takes its toll, especially for young women who find schoolwork difficult. Unless female high school graduates who are lukewarm about the prospect of more studies can be convinced that university offers a more active and self-directed form of learning, this can be an important factor in their decisions.

Still other female students who decide against university may not be turning their backs on schoolwork so much as on financial dependence. Restless with constraints on their free-dom, they are motivated by the need to earn a wage that will allow them to move away from home. Whether the pressure toward independence stems from family dynamics or is simply a normal phase of personal growth, they choose work following high school as a means of escape. To go on to

EATING THE WEDDING GIFTS

university would throw them back into dependence on parents, closing the door on that escape route unless funds miraculously fall from the sky. Putting the goal of full autonomy on hold has pay-offs only in the long run and, when personal pressures of the moment are large as life, the future can seem a long way away.

Looking to resolve problems of the present, many female high school graduates choose work to escape family constraints, unaware that the work alternative has a new set of constraints on personal growth. The mind-numbing damage of a typical unskilled job held by women sometimes takes a while to make itself known to the young woman working as a cashier, waitress, clerk, or other job holder in the service sector. The simple reason is that an unused and unchallenged brain stops processing much of anything, even Red Alerts about its own deterioration. And recall, many of these female workers were outperforming males academically only a short time earlier.

Having traded the pressure of living with parents for the boredom of low-wage work, many women soon look around for yet another way out. Why not the challenge of marriage and motherhood? Surely this is the ultimate dream of every woman.

It is not entirely accurate to suggest that young women may choose marriage as an escape from boredom. This is not the whole story—women choose relationships with men that have nothing to do with escape but everything to do with sexual attraction and romantic love. Romantic love is alive and well in our modern culture. Consider the movie plots summarized over the course of one weekend in the TV guide: *London widow loves sea captain's ghost; Slain yuppie reaches his lover with psychic's help; Subway clerk falls for comatose man's brother; An executive and a woman negotiate personal ties; Hotshot Navy jet pilot downs MIGs, loves astrophysicist; Woman seeking romance finds mercenary training camp; Hit man meets prom date ten years later; A long-nosed fire chief woos an astronomy student.*

barbara murphy

An important distinction is that, unlike their mothers and grandmothers, today's generation of young women can now enjoy romantic relationships while putting marriage and motherhood on hold. It is a sad fact, however, that women in unchallenging jobs may choose to propel their relationships into marriage in an effort to make one part of their lives more interesting.

A whole army of bridal consultants awaits young women looking for this kind of excitement. One issue of the semi-annual magazine *Today's Bride*, for example, offer 16 articles on planning the perfect wedding, including tips on the proper invitations, the wedding cake, table centrepieces, guest gifts, and music; 12 articles making sure the beautiful bride will really *be* beautiful by offering advice on make-up, hair treatment, fragrance, skin care, nail enamel, fitness and diet; 10 articles on fashion with, among other things, the editors' choice of the latest in leading-edge bridal gowns; 14 articles on the honeymoon providing details on such destinations as the Fiji Islands, St. Maarten, Australia, Barbados, Mexico, and Hawaii; 11 articles on the new matrimonial home and elegant entertaining with fine crystal, china, and silver flatware (all anticipated wedding gifts, see Bridal Registry below); and finally three articles for the groom—his wedding suit, his skill in wrapping his future bride's gift, his feeling that he is playing second fiddle in the wedding preparations (why on earth would he think that?), and other important things.

Sandwiched in among all these is additional advice for the bride on how to keep a wedding diary and, for both the bride and groom, on how to keep romance alive after setting up house. There is even an article on *second* weddings, mercifully without any tasteless reference to whatever happened to the *first*.

And these are just the articles! *Today's Bride* also contains fully 228 pages of advertisements covering the same bridal needs: invitations, centrepieces, beauty products, crystal, china patterns, flatware, and other honeymoon destinations besides those the editors have already recommended.

EATING THE WEDDING GIFTS

The crowning glory of the advertisements, however, is the array of 180 full-page photographs of stunning bridal gowns remarkably free of price tags.

And *Today's Bride* doesn't forget the wedding guests. Most of the major retailers take the opportunity to advertise their Bridal Registry, the modern version of the old haphazard custom where guests gave whatever wedding gift they felt like. One advertiser of fine china provides a convenient check list for the Bridal Registry, 102 different sizes, shapes, and specifications the bride may want in dinnerware, crystal, flatware, serving dishes, houseware, and cookware, including a column to check off whether the item was received and whether a thank-you note has been written. Putting an end to haphazard gift-giving, the Registry allows the bride to organize the generosity of hundreds of guests.

How can a young woman in her twenties who spends seven or eight hours a day working as a cashier or a waitress resist these 392 pages of gowns and gifts, images that lift her out of the tedium of her dead-end job with a promise of making her "queen for a day?" The answer is many can't resist, with rather remarkable statistics making the point. Surveying its own readers and web-site users, *Today's Bride* finds it is not the only bridal magazine reaching out to young women. Over 72 percent of those surveyed buy three or more such magazines. And, understandably, advertisers are lined up to place more ads; 80 percent of surveyed brides-to-be spend over $5,000 for that one big wedding day, half spend over $10,000. Roughly 85 percent spend over $500 on the wedding gown; almost half spend over $1,000. Unfortunately, survey questions omitted estimates on the spending of guests for that special day, but clearly the total would be substantial, enough that no retailers have been heard to say they are getting out of the wedding business.

barbara murphy

— · —

With these impressive figures from brides themselves on the average cost of a wedding, it is interesting that young women may also decide against university because of limited financial resources. In effect, they become casualties of university financing formulas which are largely dictated by government policies.

Student tuition fees have increased dramatically over the last fifteen years—affecting both males and females—as government assistance to Canadian universities has been cut back. The reduction in public funding has come after almost three decades of policies that took the opposite direction, a period when governments in most provinces attempted to make universities accessible to students at all income levels.

These earlier policies of accessibility involved, among other things, lowering the share of university costs borne by students themselves through tuition fees. From a third of university income in the post-war period, tuition fees gradually declined to 14 percent of university income on average across Canada by the early 1970s and to 9 percent by the early 1990s.[38] Governments, both federal and provincial, filled the gap that opened up as tuition fees declined. The government share grew from almost half of university income to three-quarters over the same period. Combined with government student loan programs, the goal of increased funding was greater access.

Following this period of more generous spending, government restraint policies of the past fifteen years have scuttled efforts to make universities more accessible. Tuition fees have shot up to over 17 percent (doubling the share of costs paid by students); government grants have dropped to 62 percent.[39] Students in the lowest socio-economic groups especially have shown the smallest gains in university participation.

Despite these disturbing trends, women have continued to increase their enrolment in universities across the country, somehow overcoming financial barriers. Many are clearly influenced by other, stronger motivators than tuition fee levels. As we have seen, a shift in parent expectations has taken place in recent years—parents have increasingly expected their daughters to attend university. Putting substance to these expectations parents, including parents with lower incomes, have been more willing to provide financial support to daughters as well as to sons than they did in the past. Moreover, female students, like their male counterparts, have also found their way around remaining financial barriers with their own earnings.

Looking at accessibility factors, government reviews have found that financial barriers to university enrolment are not the only barriers. Indeed in many circumstances, according to their findings, they are not the most significant barrier.[40] If the value of learning is missing, if the female student's family (like the male student's family) has not emphasized the importance of education, the likelihood of choosing university is lower whether or not financial and other barriers exist.

Young women finishing high school make important choices that will affect their lives in the short and long term. Personal goals play an important part, played out against a range of opportunities and constraints that face them in the external world. When their parents share these goals it becomes a little less difficult to find their way around obstacles that arise along the way.

Given the value that adolescents place on interpersonal concerns and their strong identification with peers, it may be surprising at first glance that young people in their teenage years are strongly influenced by their parents' opinions about higher education. It is less surprising when we realize the object of parental encouragement is not higher education for itself

barbara murphy

but higher education as the route to a career that will make the most of the special talents and abilities their children possess.

When the connection between higher education and career becomes clear to adolescents, they tend to look for advice from people in their lives who are more knowledgeable than their peers about the workings of the outside world. Increasingly, both parents are in the labour market themselves, confronting the rapidly changing job qualifications required since they went to school. Although they may seem at times to have one foot in the grave, parents are members, in fact, of the same generation as most employers. Young people finishing high school recognize that their own careers and career decisions are "adult" issues. Respect (albeit grudging respect) for adult expertise about adult matters sends them in search of consultation about higher education right in their own homes.

Just as important, consultation with parents about educational choices does not come out of the blue in the last year of high school. In most provinces key decisions about educational paths are required much earlier, some as early as middle school (or junior high) when some students are as young as 13 or 14 years. At this age students most certainly seek parental advice about program choices to be made in the four or five years of secondary school they are about to enter. And school personnel expect such consultation will take place.

Provincial departments of education claim that students are not required to make binding decisions when these secondary school choices are made at such an early age. Little research exists, however, on how many students have actually changed direction during their high school years if they found they had chosen unwisely. The process of "streaming" now used almost everywhere is intended to place students at the beginning of high school into programs with differing levels of difficulty. The objective is to offer a curriculum for each stream that is appropriate for students' post-secondary destinations, whether they be college, university, training, or direct entry into the workplace.

EATING THE WEDDING GIFTS

For young women entering high school these course choices are important decisions. The academic stream (or advanced or baccalaureate, depending on the province) is designed to provide more rigorous courses that will better prepare students for university. In choosing this stream, past academic achievement is obviously considered. Since girls have been out-performing boys at school up to these decision years, this is the logical stream for most girls. Missing this level of difficulty even for a year or two before deciding to transfer from another level means a demanding uphill climb. At 13 or 14, Canadian girls pushed or shoved into choosing the stream for university-bound students are often getting the first inkling of their parents' high expectations for them.

Four or five years later at the end of high school they are making their own mature decisions about the future against this backdrop of parental expectations. With the required course background, the decision about going to university is now their own to make. As we have seen, a resistance to more studies or a craving for financial independence are influences on some female high school students who decide instead to go directly into the work force. The assignment of women to low-wage jobs in Canada and other advanced countries is not yet a consideration in their choice; the opportunity for personal freedom looms larger. The tragic sequence that follows for some young women who then rush from a dead-end job into a marriage that fails makes high school years, when family and friends believed they were destined for great things, seem a long way off. If children are involved, the tragedy grows as young mothers become sole providers of their families, the breadwinners on some of the lowest wages in the country, and the names on very long waiting lists for government-assisted child care.

Barbara Murphy

Chapter 3

THE POVERTY OF WORKING SINGLE PARENTS

Watching the glowing bride on her wedding day, only an observer with the most terminal case of clinically diagnosed pessimism would predict that the marriage might some day break up. But for purely academic (and statistically probable) reasons, let us suppose that it does. With a rude jolt a young mother suddenly becomes the sole means of support for herself and her children unless she is lucky enough to be among the 19 percent who receive a contribution to child support from their husbands.[41]

She can spare only limited time and attention for her broken heart. If she is already working at a job requiring only high school education, she must decide if her income by itself will allow her to continue paying the rent, paying for child care, and buying groceries. Finding money for the children's clothes will have to wait. And she already knows she can count on almost a year before they outgrow what they are wearing now. Can she make it all work on less than half the family income she and her husband previously provided? While there is room for economies in much of her spending, there is little leeway on rent. The answer, therefore, is usually no.

In this hypothetical situation, let us suppose instead that the young mother can arrange child care at no cost, perhaps help from a relative or even a government-subsidized child care space. Such a fortuitous development might take some time to arrange, but in the meantime she will simply have to cut back on food. While she scrambles for solutions, there are always the wedding gifts—it is highly likely they are not edible, but selling them might bring in enough to pay for groceries over the short term.

With free child care and less spending on food, the young mother begins to provide a life for herself and her children that is drastically different from the life they had before. Searching for a better job becomes a priority but, for women, the labour market can be an unfriendly place.

When it comes to work, women seem to be assigned to a labour market on another planet—perhaps Venus, the planet that reportedly gave women life in the first place. Back here on Earth the labour market is geared to males. The pay is higher, the work more interesting, and there is little enthusiasm for changing the old hiring practices of the past century. In an effort to make things right, offices for equal employment opportunity have sprung up all across the country, dozens of affirmative action programs have been introduced, and equal pay for work of equal value has been enshrined in law.

The results are modest, at best. Some gains have been made by the increasing number of women with university degrees, but for the rest of women all these government programs have made little difference. These unlucky female workers fill a special niche in the labour market that simply reflects the needs of the economy for a supply of relatively inexpensive workers. Firmly embedded in Canada's economic structure, it is not surprising that low-wage jobs filled by women show little change over time.

The average wage of Canadian women is 64 percent of the average wage for men.[42] Although some of this gap can be explained by women's part-time work, even women working full time earn only 70 percent of what men earn, on average.

barbara murphy

Twenty years ago women's wages were only 52 percent of men's. Women have made this gain, according to Statistics Canada analysts, partly because they have invested heavily in higher education leading to jobs in higher paying occupations. Nonetheless, women with only high school education continue to pull the average female wage down to less than two-thirds of the male wage.

Most labour market researchers acknowledge that women's low wages are largely due to their segregation in low-wage sectors of the economy. Four out of five women in the labour force are concentrated in service or non-manufacturing industries, a proportion that has dramatically increased since the end of World War II.[43] Moreover, service industry jobs are more and more becoming female-designated jobs—less than 40 percent were held by women 50 years ago; today women hold over half of service industry jobs.

Parts of the service sector have even less attractive working conditions than others. Within the total group of industries that provide services rather than goods, many traditional industries rely less on technology and, despite such advances in information-based service industries, traditional industries have continued to be labour-intensive, that is, labour costs make up a high proportion of their costs. These industries, paying the lowest wages, have the highest number of female employees.

Because the service sector covers a broad range of industries from banks and insurance companies to fast food outlets, from law firms to childcare centres, the distribution of women among specific occupations gives a clearer picture of concentration. Over 50 percent of working women are office clerks, secretaries, retail sales clerks, waitresses, cashiers, or child care workers. Their concentration in these traditionally low-paid jobs explains the continuing wage gap between men and women, a gap that is only slightly offset by the concentration of women in teaching and nursing (8 percent of working women) at marginally higher salaries.[44]

EATING THE WEDDING GIFTS

Women now dominate low-wage service jobs to such an extent that they are now known as female jobs. Virtually all secretaries are women (99 percent); almost three-quarters of office clerks are women; 89 percent of cashiers and 79 percent of waitresses are women; 95 percent of child care and home support workers are women; and 62 percent of retail sales clerks are women.[45]

Given their segregation in these occupations it is not surprising that women hold two-thirds of all minimum-wage jobs in Canada. A Statistics Canada study in 2003 found that some 27,000 heads of family (mostly female) with no spouse were working for minimum wage or less.[46] Most had to support at least one child on a minimum wage that generally ran between $6 and $7 an hour in most provinces. They were concentrated in accommodation, food and retail trade jobs, jobs that are rarely unionized and carry few benefits. The study also found that minimum wage workers were not only likely to be female, they were likely to be without post-secondary education.

With these strong indications of distinct labour markets for women and men, the question of why this is so obviously arises. Now firmly a part of the economic structure, how did this division of labour develop while we all stood by?

— • —

The concentration of women workers in a low-wage sector of the labour market is not new. It has been a fact of women's employment long before labour market analysts began to identify a dual labour market in Western economies in the past quarter century. The low-wage sector of the dual labour market, it has been argued in their studies, generally includes visible minorities, women, youth, and other unskilled workers (for example, migrant workers in Europe and California) and is characterized by an absence of unions and very little mobility of workers from that sector to the high-wage sector.

barbara murphy

Women in particular have had a long history in unattractive jobs. Over a hundred years ago the concentration of women in certain jobs was a matter of little study, overshadowed by the huge social adjustment taking place as a result of women entering the labour force after centuries of staying at home. In the early years of Canada's move to an industrial economy, young daughters of wage workers and farmers left their homes to find work in the small factories that began to operate in urban centres. Despite society's view of the frailty of women, they were found to be quite capable of performing the simple repetitive tasks of labour-intensive industries where seasonal work and piecework were mechanisms for keeping costs down.

For employers in these industries women were a cheap and compliant work force. Census figures for 1901 show that most female factory workers were concentrated in the garment industry where their work as dressmakers and seamstresses involved long hours and low wages.[47] If garment trade employers were called upon to justify the low wages—and they rarely were—they pointed out that women's wages were not meant to provide for a whole family, as men's were. The wages of wives and daughters were meant merely to supplement those of the male breadwinner. And furthermore, there was nothing in their qualifications to warrant higher wages. Women, it was argued, brought no skills to the garment industry that were not part of the natural skills all women used in the home.

There were other early concentrations of working women. At the turn of the century many Canadian women were in teaching, a field they had entered as far back as pre-Confederation years when most teachers were male. The wages of teachers were even lower than those of female factory workers, yet the social status of teachers had gradually risen over the years. As a result many young women of a new generation intent on joining the labour force to gain financial independence chose the respectability of teaching over the questionable prestige of factory work.

EATING THE WEDDING GIFTS

By 1900 women dominated the teaching profession. In a half century they had grown from less than 25 percent of teachers in Ontario to 75 percent.[48] Over the same period, however, this shift allowed local school boards to pay consistently low wages, justifying them by the short term women were expected to teach before marriage. Once again the skills that women brought to their labour force work were considered natural, if not innate. Didn't it make sense that young women—Canada's future mothers who would be responsible for the basic instruction of small children as they reared their own families—would be best suited for teaching society's young?

School boards paid lip service to these important female talents, but even as women became the majority of teachers they were paid less than male teachers (from 50 to 75 percent less) and few women would become school principals for another 75 years.

Women entering the labour force at the turn of the century could also choose nursing. Indeed, nursing was the most female-dominated of all occupations; all nurses were women. With medical services increasingly centralized in hospitals in the late 19th century, Canadian women from urban working-class families, from small towns, and from farms readily provided a labour force for hospital boards who were as intent on containing costs as were school boards. These arrangements were calling nursing schools,[49] two-year training programs based on practical nursing experience in the hospital. In many cases unpaid student nurses made up the entire hospital nursing staff.

During these two years of unpaid hospital work (only 12 percent of training hours were devoted to lectures), the stage was set for nurses to regard their employment as a noble calling. After graduation they worked for low wages either in hospitals or private homes, their work considered a public service, a labour of love, and a fitting use of the nurturing skills that came so naturally to women. There were even suggestions that nurses themselves came out ahead—according to

barbara murphy

the 1916 Ontario Commission on Unemployment, they were better fitted for marriage by virtue of the training they had received in health care, diet, and cleanliness, among other things.

In the late 19th century, small factory work, teaching, or nursing were the limited choices open to women who were looking for paid work but were unwilling to take the only other option—domestic work in a private home. Within a short time, however, new opportunities for women opened up in a new white-collar sector of the labour market. White-collar or office work became an expanding field as the Canadian economy moved from primary industries to manufacturing, from small businesses to large corporations, and from basic bookkeeping tasks (usually carried out by a male bookkeeper anticipating upward mobility within the organization) to complex administrative systems that required a greater number of office workers to process an increasing amount of paper work. This new need for office work heralded the growth of large armies of clerical workers, almost all women, that would become a permanent fixture of corporations and governments over the next hundred years. From comprising two percent of the total labour force in 1891, clerical workers grew to 16 percent of the total labour force and 30 percent of the female labour force by the end of the 20th century.[50]

Historians of the revolution that took place in offices in Canada and other industrial countries point to a number of reasons why it was women rather than men who came to fill these jobs. From the mainly solitary bookkeeping jobs of the 19th century that were filled by men, the composition of the clerical work force shifted to female jobs, and today almost 80 percent are held by women. One contributing factor was the new entry of women into the labour force just as administrative work in the economy was beginning to grow. Female wages were only half of male wages for reasons that we have seen—women were not considered principal breadwinners for the family. As a result, employers reaped the benefits of low-wage workers in a new part of their operations that required expansion. At the same time they restructured the earlier bookkeeping tasks performed by men by breaking them down into simple routines, requiring few skills, and lending themselves to easy regulation and supervision, all of which could be performed by women with no illusions of upward mobility in the organization.

Once women were fitted into these slots it became difficult to change the size and shape of the slots over the years, and certainly employers had no incentive to change them. In fact, there was every reason to make clerical jobs more and more suitable for women who, it was assumed, were only tentatively attached to the labour force while awaiting marriage and motherhood. While the monotony of routine work suited the short-term employment of women, it was happily discarded by young men as a necessary step to advancement. Formally or not, employers began to put into practice a division of labour that placed men in jobs that required stability, long tenure, and adequate wages consistent with their career aspirations as family heads, and placed women in jobs that were characterized by instability and low wages.

There is less history to tell about the concentration of women in service jobs. For one thing, service industries only began to make an impact on the economy after World War II when Canada and other advanced countries moved toward what has been called a post-industrial economy. Service industries, or non-manufacturing industries, began to represent a larger and larger share of the Gross Domestic Product in Canada over the next 50 years; today the service sector contributes two-thirds of Canada's GDP. It also provides most of the country's jobs—in the early part of the 20th century only one in three Canadians was employed in the service sector while today three of every four have service sector jobs.[51]

This dramatic shift to a service economy had a number of causes. The proportion of Canadian workers in primary industries, for example, agriculture, fishing, logging, and mining, fell in the post-war period and continued to fall until the end of the century. In manufacturing, technological

barbara murphy

advances by the 1950s began to bring about substantial increases in productivity and substantial decreases in the number of workers needed for the same levels of output. And at the same time as some industries were becoming more automated, many of those industries in Canada that remained labour-intensive were lost to other countries. These changes in the goods-producing sector of the economy translated into no growth in direct manufacturing jobs while services in support of producing goods (financial, insurance, legal, and others) were on the rise.

Shifts in Canadian public spending priorities were also reflected in increased spending in health, education, and public administration, for the most part related to job growth.

Demographic changes and lifestyle changes also contributed to the growth of the service sector. By the 1960s women were entering the labour force in increasing numbers. The work they traditionally performed in the home at no cost to the economy was gradually picked up by new service industries at a cost. Moreover, as more women worked and two-income families became the norm, more Canadians could afford to eat out, send laundry out, travel, and spend more time in leisure activities, all of which contributed to a growth in services to support these new lifestyles.

The timing of service sector growth was, therefore, both cause and effect of the growth of the female labour force. It is difficult to say with certainty which came first. It was not enough for women to decide to leave their homes; there had to be jobs for them to go to. With no growth in manufacturing jobs and new growth in service sector jobs it is not surprising that women streamed into service jobs. What is more interesting is that within the service sector, which is divided into high tech and low tech industries, women tend to be concentrated at the low tech end of the ladder.

Some of this concentration is due to the relatively lower levels of education of the first streams of women in the

1960s, which restricted them to traditional service jobs in food and accommodation services or in retail stores. As well, attitudes about women as secondary wage earners had not changed, and wages were set lower accordingly. As with clerical workers, no amount of employment equity legislation has been able to un-stick this deeply rooted practice of relegating women to low-wage ghettos in service industries.

Today these jobs are women's jobs, dead-end jobs with no opportunity for promotion. A growing number are also part-time jobs, usually defined as those with less than 30 working hours per week. While some workers prefer part-time work for personal reasons, the Economic Council of Canada points out that nearly half of new part-time jobs created in Canada are classified as "involuntary" part-time, that is, workers would have preferred full-time jobs if they could have found them.[52] The Council's report, *Good Jobs, Bad Jobs*, notes that most part-time workers are employed in the low tech end of the service sector and the overwhelming majority are either young or female, or both.

The higher education levels of a new generation of women seeking more attractive positions[53] may force employers in the low end of the service sector to balance the gender composition of the jobs, both full- and part-time, in their industries. In the meantime, however, restaurant, hotel, and retail jobs are the destination for many women with high school education looking for work.

— • —

The origins of low-wage female job ghettos throw some light on their tendency to remain a permanent feature of the economic structure over the years despite recent gains made by many working women. The young mother, however, who finds herself making ends meet after separation or divorce will receive little comfort from an explanation of how her assignment to the bottom of the labour market all began. The reality for her is the poverty of her family today and the

barbara murphy

complete absence of any hope for the future to be found in her dead-end job.

It has been a somewhat different reality for women in the Canadian labour force who are in mainstream occupations. Women have made inroads in some areas, especially over the past 30 years, with results that begin to show in the male-female wage gap. These women, if left on their own with young children to support, are not suffering the same hardships as their counterparts in female job ghettos. It is true that family income drops for women in mainstream occupations after marriage breakdown as it does for women in segregated occupations, but it does not drop so dramatically far.

Over 30 years, while women have continued their domination of clerical and service jobs, new entries into the labour force have been branching out. As a result changes are taking place in the way women are distributed across a number of other occupations. By the end of the century a greater proportion of working women were in managerial jobs than ever before. It was not a world-shattering proportion, but it had shown a slow, steady climb from two percent to eight percent of all working women.[54] Some of this quadrupling was due to a greater number of managerial jobs in general, but women were getting a greater share of new managerial jobs than their share of the total work force.

In the 1990s men still held 60 percent of managerial occupations in Canada, but this was a long way from the 84 percent they held in the 1970s.[55] Over 400,000 new women managers had changed the picture, moving themselves into occupations that were ranked among the ten highest-paying in the country.

The changed distribution of the female labour force also showed more women in occupations in natural sciences, engineering, and mathematics, where the portion of women choosing such careers tripled. While this occupational group moved only slightly over 30 years, its movement was upward, and women made up most of the growth. Near the end of the century 20 percent of scientists, engineers, and mathematicians were women compared to only seven percent 30 years earlier. Almost 100,000 new women workers had entered the field. Women and mathematics? They had come a long way from the dire warnings of 19th-century physicians that women's physiology was simply not organized for the strain of brain work.

In other areas of the labour market women also increased their representation over the same period. They grew from a minority of 37 percent to a majority of 61 percent of all workers in the social science field. In addition, with women making up the majority of graduating classes in law and medicine, there were an increasing number of female lawyers and doctors. A growing portion of working women were also found in artistic, literary, and recreation jobs.

Although women making inroads into male-dominated occupations are rewarded with higher wages, they find other job advantages related to their own personal development that appeal to them as much as, if not more than, financial rewards. First on the list for most women is the use of their intellect, their creativity, and their interpersonal skills that they would not find in the routine jobs most women are assigned to or in the traditional work women have done in the home (and which they will still have to tackle on weekends).

Almost as important is their greater ability to regulate their own work hours and to choose methods of carrying out their work that are based on their own individual assessment of what will work best, and not based on pre-arranged procedures set by someone else. All these advantages add up to greater control and decision-making power, something notably missing in dead-end jobs.

Job descriptions highlight the differences in more concrete terms. Managers are expected, among other things, "to develop marketing plans,"[56] a clear expectation that managers will be creative enough and intelligent enough to dream up appropriate strategies and put them on paper. They are also expected "to maintain and develop business relationships,"

barbara murphy

anticipating that they can work harmoniously and productively with others, something normally not required in the daily workload of a clerk faced with a stack of invoices to be processed. Managers must "motivate staff to ensure the profitability of sales," a standard phrase that means managers must have special skills in developing the full potential of others as compared with the normal requirement of most female low-wage jobs to carry out one's duties (and certainly no more) and leave others to theirs.

Job descriptions for retail sales clerks, cashiers, and waitresses leave little room for such decision-making or control of tasks. Retail sales clerks "greet customers, discuss merchandise, assist in setting out merchandise for display, wrap purchases, direct customers to product locations, and perform various tidying and cleaning tasks." While these tasks do not require creativity, initiative, or skills in getting the best out of other workers, they do require communication and interpersonal skills in "greeting customers" and "discussing merchandise," skills that are highly likely to be related to final sales. Despite this obviously strong relationship, retail clerks are not well paid. Their low wages combined with the lack of control over their work ultimately erode the one important asset they bring to this kind work, their ability to initiate and successfully sustain the only personal contact retail employers have with their customers.

General office clerks "prepare correspondence, operate office machines, answer telephone calls, photocopy, file, handle incoming and outgoing mail and faxes, and prepare invoices." Most clerks would agree—and recall, a high school diploma is a prerequisite, a diploma that requires completion of difficult and exacting courses in all provinces of Canada—that none of the above clerical duties challenges their intellect. Nor do the duties require creativity or motivational skills. It is true that a minimal amount of interpersonal skills would be required in answering the telephone, but the duties that take up most of the day are so routine that many an office clerk almost prays for the telephone to ring.

EATING THE WEDDING GIFTS

Waitresses "greet patrons, present menus, take orders and relay to kitchen staff, serve food, present bills and accept payments." Cashiers "identify the price of the product, receive payment, wrap or bag merchandise, total sales on completion of the work shift, and [like the retail sales clerk who is also female with traditional female domestic skills] keep the work area clean." Waitresses and cashiers, in particular, have little control over the pace of their work and take no part in decisions about how it might best be performed.

The lack of challenge in jobs for high school graduates is destructive in the sense that many young women stop using their intellectual machinery and fail to develop their potential. Moreover, they finally lose interest in doing anything about it. So many factors in their daily work environment tell them they are of limited value to their employers and to society that they come to believe they are capable of performing no more than the most routine of tasks. The days they most enjoy are the days off work.

Other women workers, those who are being challenged daily by job requirements that allow them the full use of their talents, are happily employed. Better pay is certainly satisfying, but so is the feeling of self-worth that comes with meeting challenges.

These are the personal growth differences between the two groups of working women, aside from the very real economic differences that separate them. If they are supporting children on their own, both personal and economic self-sufficiency are important to their own feelings of worth and to the health and personal well-being of the children completely dependent on them.

Barbara Murphy

Chapter 4

THE POVERTY OF SINGLE PARENTS ON WELFARE

Society has mixed messages for the divorced mother who tries to keep a job when she has young children. She's damned if she does, and she's damned if she doesn't. On the one hand, she can choose to keep her job and find someone else to care for her children, for which decision she can be pilloried for neglect or, at the very least, for contributing to society's future juvenile delinquents. On the other hand, she can choose to stay at home to look after her own children while she supports her family on welfare, an option that brings another form of criticism from a demanding (and distrustful) society that labels all those out of the work force as malingerers.

Not too many years ago the second of these choices was held to be the more socially acceptable. Separated, divorced, or widowed mothers were expected to care for their own children. They were not urged to go to work; indeed they were not particularly welcome in the work force. What began as pensions for mothers raising children on their own in the early 20th century were meant to make it possible for them to stay at home. Mothers' pensions continued under a variety of program names specific to each province for most of the century and never lost their main thrust as a means of ensuring children were cared for by their own mothers. Nor did society's value system waver significantly from this emphasis. Children cared for in this traditional way, it was believed, would receive the best kind of care and were less likely to become a burden on society later.

More recently social attitudes have changed. We worry less about the potential delinquency of children (or that particular concern has been lost in a trade-off) and more about the potential burden on society of unemployed mothers who, many people suspect, will lose their incentive to work if they are given "hand-outs" in the form of welfare payments. To bring about this new and presumably more productive approach, governments will provide low-cost child care that will be every bit as good for the child as a mother's care, and perhaps even better. In other words, child care by someone other than the mother, formerly a bad thing, is now a good thing. It has been a remarkable transformation, and young mothers of a new generation of single parents line up for the low-cost child care that society has now deemed to be the answer to all their problems.

Unfortunately, access to low-cost child care has proven to be an illusion. It may be useful to look at the many obstacles that still stand in its way before looking at the logical out-come—in the absence of childcare, many single parents cannot hold a job and end up on welfare. Moreover, while the income from a clerical or service sector job may be low, as we have seen, the income from a monthly welfare allowance is inordinately lower.

The obstacles to finding low-cost child care are common to almost every province and territory in Canada. With even the most basic requirements of safety, it is not feasible for child care centres to provide care at low cost—child care staff are already among the lowest-paid workers in the country. Monthly child care fees can run from $380 a month in New Brunswick to $780 a month in Ontario.[57] This range represents

barbara murphy

close to half the take-home pay of many clerical and service workers. Low-cost child care is only a reality when governments provide for the cost of a child's care, either in full or in part, and governments have not come close to providing such funds for all children of working mothers who are also single parents. It is the major missing piece in society's new solution to keeping mothers off welfare. Not only is there a drastic shortage of funding for child care, but single parents continue to receive the same pressure about going to work as if the funding were available.

There are roughly five million children under 12 years of age in Canada, of whom a little over three million (or almost two-thirds) are children of working mothers.[58] Most of these children are cared for in informal arrangements that do not involve provincial governments in either licensing or funding. Only a small percentage, averaging 12 percent across Canada, are in licensed, or regulated, child care programs. In turn, only a little over a third of children in these regulated spaces receive government assistance with child care fees.[59] Given that government assistance is provided only to families in the greatest financial need in every province but Quebec (see below), it is probably safe to assume that most of the children whose fees are fully or partly subsidized are children of single parents.

With these numbers, even the roughest of calculations points out the difficulties for single parents looking for government-subsidized child care. Over 600,000 Canadian single parents with children under ten are competing for roughly 130,000 subsidized spaces; 470,000 will be disappointed.[60] Most single parents who have already experienced these odds first hand would have little need for statistics to convince them that low-cost government-subsidized child care is a distant dream.

Is the situation likely to improve? Many parents and child care advocacy groups have struggled with this issue for almost three decades. A review of developments in a few of the provinces tells the story.

Over the past 20 years Nova Scotia working parents have watched the halting growth of public funding for child care, most of which has been dedicated to subsidizing the fees of low-income parents. Nova Scotia, whose poor families represent 15 percent of all families in the province (close to the national average), has also allocated funding directly to child care centres for the purpose of improving staff salaries and upgrading each centre's physical equipment.

The provincial government funds a total of 2,655 subsidized spaces in regulated child care programs. In addition, it pays for the child care (often informal arrangements) of another 550 children whose parents take part in employment-readiness programs while on social assistance. This means that Nova Scotia single parents who are already working and hoping to stay off social assistance will apply for one of the subsidized spaces in licensed child care programs. Unfortunately, these parents have among them a total of over 7,000 children under 12 years of age to try to squeeze into the 2,655 spaces.[61]

The situation is almost as bad in Ontario. While the provincial government there spent $300 million on child care fee subsidies in 2001, or enough for an estimated 76,000 children, there are over 100,000 children under 12 whose parents are single and work full-time. Like Nova Scotia, Ontario also pays for child care costs in informal arrangements when parents are in employment programs to help them leave social assistance and participate in the work force.

Working parents in Ontario have also watched with dismay the slowing down of growth in the number of subsidized child care spaces over the past five years. When new funds finally materialized they were diverted elsewhere. Over $114 million in new funding originating from a federal-provincial agreement and earmarked for early childhood programs has been spent by the provincial government on a variety of other social services, most of which are not related to child care.

barbara murphy

Many single parents in Saskatchewan are also affected by a shortage of low-cost child care. Saskatchewan, with its relatively large rural population and its high proportion of Aboriginal families, provides funding in problem areas that are not necessarily related to the needs of working parents. With child care funding dispersed in this way, over 9,000 children under 12 of single parents working full-time are far more than can be accommodated in the 3,600 subsidized spaces in regular child care centres, a number that has not grown over the last ten years.

Alberta has reduced its subsidized child care spaces since the mid-1990s. The number of fee subsidies dropped by almost 20 percent between 1995 and 2001, leaving some 20,000 children under 12 of working single parents trying to access 10,000 spaces.

Over the same period working parents in B.C. have seen five separate government ministries in succession involved in child care administration with funding changes that are difficult to follow. For the most part, funding has been cut in many areas. By 2001 the government estimated that 18,500 children were subsidized by direct grants to child care centres throughout the province. According to Statistics Canada figures on working single parents in B.C., this number of spaces left over 11,000 children under 12 still looking for subsidized child care.

Over the last seven or eight years Quebec has spent its child care dollars in quite a different way. Every child in the province is now eligible for government assistance for child care to the extent that all parents who can find a space pay a maximum daily rate that is only a fraction of the cost of the service. Single parents with low incomes pay even less. Although single parents are not necessarily given priority as spaces become available, individual child care programs may have such a policy.

A major expansion of child care has taken place in the province over this period, doubling the number of regular spaces, but without a priority system the effect on single parents is not known. A total of 770,000 children in Quebec had working mothers in 2001; a total of 235,000 child care spaces were covered by public funds.

These examples of provincial child care shortages illustrate the difficulties many Canadian single parents face in trying to keep their jobs. Successive governments at the federal level (led by two different political parties in turn) have promised to improve the picture nationally by providing child care funds to the provinces to allow for a more universally available system. Sadly, this national expansion has not taken place.

The most recent federal government has promised a massive infusion of funds to create a model across the country similar to the universal model in Quebec. In full operation such a national system would help all working parents. However, while universality gives recognition to the needs of two-parent families more than ever before, it leaves single parents competing for spaces in a larger arena, especially during a start-up period when spaces are being added only as new funding permits (and recall that there are over three million children of working mothers in Canada today and only 400,000 are covered by existing public funds). In the long run, a universal system would resemble the education system with the same advantages for all Canada's children. In the short run, single parents are not necessarily the parent group that would see a great deal of change.

At present female single parents are facing shortages everywhere in Canada. Economic researchers who have studied the job decisions of single parents have found the effects of child care costs (and availability) are strong.[62] Indeed, when marriages break down and female single parents make decisions about employment, child care costs are often the deciding factor in their calculations. If a government-subsidized space is not available, many find they cannot afford the additional cost on top of rent and groceries, especially when their high school education restricts them to low wages. They leave their jobs and turn to social assistance for the financial support they need for their families.

barbara murphy

— • —

Welfare is the last resort for single parents unable to find low-cost child care that would allow them to keep working. Almost a quarter of Canadian single parents end up taking this step.[63] And as the rate of marriage breakdown has risen over the last 20 years they have accounted for a larger and larger proportion of the welfare caseload. In the late 1990s over 40 percent of all individuals receiving welfare across the country were mothers and children in single-parent families.[64]

Although welfare may be their last resort, most single parents are not prepared for the limited income it provides. Welfare allowances in Canada are meant to provide only the basic necessities of life—food, clothing, and rent—to people who have exhausted all other means of income. Even after the most superficial examination of provincial welfare allowances, however, this intention has to be dismissed as purely theoretical. Rather than using a realistic measure of necessities, most provinces peg their welfare allowances slightly below minimum wage levels for obvious reasons of avoiding disincentives to work. As we have seen, minimum wages of $6 and $7 an hour in Canada leave workers short of money for either food or rent costs (forget about clothing), and many minimum wage workers have to hold more than one job to make ends meet.[65] Pegging provincial welfare rates even lower than minimum wages means Canadians have to be really desperate before they resort to welfare.

An alarming indication of what it's like to live on welfare are the reports of Canadian food banks that 57 percent of their customers are receiving social assistance.[66] Moreover, most families visiting food banks are single-parent families (almost two-thirds). The average customer depends on the food bank once or twice a month, and the average hamper taken away is four days' worth of food. Food banks, which first appeared in Canada in the early 1980s as a temporary measure, are now a permanent fixture in Canadian cities. Over seven million pounds of food are distributed each month, of which roughly four million are going to people who cannot make ends meet on provincial welfare allowances.

One of the most significant factors accounting for the inadequacy of welfare rates that sends so many to food banks is the high cost of rent across the country. Monthly welfare allowances are generally made up of two parts: an allowance for shelter costs (the maximum allotted by the government for rent) and an allowance for all other necessities including food, clothing, and other essentials. In most provinces the shelter allowance is so far out of line with actual rents landlords are charging that families on welfare are forced to cut deep into their food allowance to find the money for rent. A few examples give the general picture.

In Nova Scotia the shelter allowance is $550 a month for a single parent with one child.[67] Rents for a two-bedroom apartment in Halifax, however, average $653 a month.[68] Saskatchewan single parents with one child are allowed a maximum of $385 a month for shelter in the larger centres of Regina, Saskatoon and others,[69] while the 2002 rents in those cities averaged $550.

The shelter allowance for a single parent with one child in Ontario is $511[70]; the average rent in Toronto is $982 and in Ottawa, $888. Even a one-bedroom apartment in Toronto (a possibility for a few single parents, depending on the age and sex of the child) is rented for $832 on average; in Ottawa, for $731. In both cities these average rents are not only higher than the shelter allowance, they are higher than the total monthly welfare payment which is also meant to cover food and clothing. Some may be lucky enough to access public housing (but their shelter allowance will be lowered), and many are also making a home for themselves and their children in emergency shelters.

Outside Toronto and Ottawa, single parents in Ontario fare a little better with average rents ranging from $609 in Sarnia to $842 in Barrie—in all urban areas, however, rents run considerably higher than the provincial shelter allowance of $511.

barbara murphy

In Calgary the shelter allowance for a single parent with one child is $482 a month;[71] the average rent in that city is $753 for two bedrooms. In Edmonton the situation is slightly better at $600 for rent in 2002, on average. Like Toronto and Ottawa, Calgary has average rents that are greater than the total monthly welfare payment for single parents, including their allowances for food and clothing.

In Vancouver, where rents are among the highest in the country, single parents on welfare are in the same situation as their counterparts in Toronto, Ottawa, and Calgary. The B.C. government's total monthly welfare allowance, including the amount meant for food, fails to cover even the rent.

With this bleak accommodation situation across the country, surprisingly few single parents have been able to move in with family or relatives. Their parents, it appears, are not rattling around in excess living space they don't need and few are welcoming back their separate or divorced offspring with open arms. Despite high rents, only one percent of single parents on welfare in Canada live with relatives.[72]

Explanations for government policies that set shelter allowances far below average rents in most parts of Canada are hard to come by. Understandably, families in receipt of government assistance are expected to search for accommodation in the low end of the rental market. Unfortunately, when the market is tight, vacancies at the low end are almost non-existent. What may appear logical in theory becomes impossible in reality. When single-parent families (and indeed all families) on welfare use food allowances to bolster up shelter allowances, they have the option of turning to food banks or going hungry. The impact on children is the greatest cause for concern. Over a million Canadian children depend on welfare incomes; three-quarters of them are the children of single parents and many are going hungry during parts of each month.

With clear evidence in mounting poverty figures that many welfare parents in all provinces were cutting into their food budgets, concern about hungry children brought in new measures in the 1990s with the introduction of federal child tax benefits for low-income families. While the new benefits have become a source of income for parents to turn to for food, they fall short in their objective of eliminating child poverty. Welfare single parents are still left with incomes far below the poverty line. Their incomes including child tax benefits range from 49 percent of the poverty line in Alberta to 73 percent in Newfoundland, with the combined incomes of child tax benefits and welfare in most provinces averaging 60 percent.[73]

If shortfalls in rent are coming out of provincial food allowances and if federal child benefits replace only a small part of the shortfall, just how badly off are welfare parents and their children when it comes to food on the table? Like rents, grocery costs vary considerably across the country so comparisons of how well provincial welfare rates cover food costs are difficult. With this in mind, the federal government has developed a new tool for measuring what it costs to buy basic necessities including food, shelter, transportation and other household goods and services. Called the Market Basket Measure, it estimates the minimum income a family needs to pay for essential living costs in each area of the country. As we have seen, welfare families are falling short of income for rent, given real average rents across all provinces. The Market Basket Measure, which also estimates the other essentials, completes the picture.

Social Planning Councils in both Edmonton and Vancouver have made comparisons with the federal Market Basket Measure and found welfare rates in Alberta and B.C. falling far short of the minimum required. Even adding in federal child tax benefits, Edmonton single-parent welfare families fell 20 percent short of Market Basket thresholds; Vancouver single-parent families fell 25 percent short. A similar comparison by the Social Planning Council of Toronto found welfare families in Toronto were living on 43 percent less than the Market Basket Measure estimate of income required for basic essentials, even when child tax benefits were included.

barbara murphy

Despite these new calculations that show so many families living below an estimated rock-bottom minimum, welfare rates are low and are likely to remain low because of shifts in public attitudes and values in the last decade. Not many in the new century are championing the cause of Canadians on public assistance. The whole idea of helping dependent people has come under fire as Canadian citizens concerned about taxes and deficits and public debt have found it unpalatable to help those who cannot help themselves.

Reflecting these changing attitudes, new negative stereotypes of Canadians receiving welfare have become accepted truths. For the most part they are based on what the National Council of Welfare confirms are myths about welfare, but nonetheless they have become popular and go a long way toward justifying the philosophy that the poor bring about their own misfortune and, therefore, they are not deserving of society's help.

Harsher attitudes about less fortunate Canadians have been reflected in changing government policies. In the 1990s many provincial governments brought in what was heralded as "welfare reform." If welfare recipients for a fleeting moment understood this to mean more realistic welfare allowances, they were soon to learn otherwise. Public assistance programs were overhauled with a brand new emphasis on getting people to work, almost as if that was never the goal of those who unfortunately found themselves on welfare. Allowances were cut (because the new stereotype was a welfare recipient wasting his or her allowance on beer and cigarettes), welfare applicants were told payments would be stopped if they failed to take training or employment (the new stereotype was an idler not wanting to work and choosing instead to enjoy life on a generous welfare allowance), and many dollars were spent on looking for fraud (the new stereotype was a dishonest person receiving welfare while he or she really held a well-paid full-time job).

In this new atmosphere single parents, earlier regarded as unemployable because of child care responsibilities, became employable overnight. Funds became available for them to pay child caregivers or babysitters so they could train or search for work. With offers of no-cost child care, many who had gone on welfare because they couldn't get subsidized care for their children while they worked must have found their heads spinning. They could not really be blamed for complaining that, although free child care was a goal now realized, the only problem was you had to go on welfare to get it.

Demanding landlords, low shelter allowances, tight food budgets, and monthly (or more) food bank visits are some of the major pressures on female single parents on welfare. But most will concede these are not as difficult to cope with as the lowered value, even disapproval, placed on their children and themselves by neighbours, merchants, the school system, the media, the welfare office, and the larger community. They would have a difficult time identifying precisely the many ways Canadians deliver these messages of reproach and blame. The messages are real nonetheless.

One single parent, presenting a welfare food voucher at a supermarket to pay for a cart of groceries, had to wait while the cashier called across three check-out counters to another cashier: "Do these welfare people pay sales tax?" Another could not persuade her daughter to take a note to school asking for financial assistance for a fairly costly field trip. Her daughter pleaded: "Just let me stay home that day. I have to take the note to the office and everyone will know." Another single parent claimed that a home visit from the social worker was more humiliating than having a police car at your door.

In a hundred different ways these single parents and their children live with the stigma of being on welfare in Canada. Trips to the food bank are seen as an indication of ineptness in managing what many contend are perfectly adequate welfare budgets, buying Pampers diapers a sign of wasteful spending just for the mother's convenience. To counter this mismanagement many welfare departments will not entrust recipients with shelter allowances, their rents instead going directly to the landlord. Reinforcing the stereotype of welfare squandering, one provincial premier justified cutting back a pregnancy allowance of $37

Barbara Murphy

a month to pregnant mothers on welfare by stating: "What we are making sure is that those dollars don't go to beer."[74]

So great is the perception of waste and fraud that public pressure has grown since the 1990s to make the fingerprinting of welfare applicants mandatory. In addition, some provincial governments with considerable public support have hired welfare inspectors to get financial information from banks and to ask neighbours, landlords, or clerks at the corner store about personal living arrangements of people on welfare.

Sadly, welfare recipients have also passed over into the realm of humour, becoming the butts of presumably clever jokes by many members of the media, prompting Janice Kennedy of the *Ottawa Citizen* to write:

> ... the art of poor-mocking is more than simply fun. It can double as a superb marginalization tool, a powerful strategy for anyone looking to de-humanize, demonize and dismiss those people littering the path to the shining goal: deficit-busting, tax reduction and justifying the morally unjustifiable.[75]

Humour and ridicule are only some of the methods society can use to label some of its members. With very little humour governments have in recent years announced brand new measures to curb the waste and dishonesty of welfare recipients without first providing a shred of satisfactory evidence that waste and dishonesty exist. These announcements become successful strategies for the perpetuation of stereotypes in that no right-thinking Canadian can imagine their government would propose elaborate solutions if there were not real problems. Unfortunately, because labels and stereotypes are so much easier to understand, many fail to examine the accuracy of the original premise.

— • —

After marriage break-up a young mother, now suddenly on her own, can barely give attention to her emotional needs before she is forced into decisions about how she will provide for her family. With a low-paying job and a shortage of affordable child care, it is an uphill struggle. What is continually surprising is that so many fight these battles with quiet determination. We rarely hear from the sole providers of single-parent families because we rarely ask. And we rarely ask because, in our more honest moments, we know we won't like what we hear.

Barbara Murphy

Chapter 5

LOW-INCOME SINGLE PARENTS, THEIR STORIES

Every female single parent has a unique story. The circumstances that led each one into a marriage that didn't last are as varied as their own personal backgrounds from childhood through teenage years. Similarly, the events that led to marriage breakdown are different in each story—some single parents experienced physical abuse during marriage though many did not, some found their husbands unwilling to take on adult responsibilities, some concede their own judgment in choosing a partner was far from sound, and some simply cannot explain why their marriage deteriorated. Despite these different scenarios, however, some very typical experiences follow the break-up of a marriage.

Most of the single parents interviewed for this chapter received no child support following separation. With no means of providing for themselves and their children, they applied for government social assistance. Many held part-time jobs while on assistance, the work hours restricted by the need to be at home with children and the work itself uninspiring.

The drudgery of unchallenging work can sometimes breed resentment aimed at the very people a single parent is trying to support financially. Debra, who has taken cleaning jobs to supplement welfare payments, complains about her children: "I work hard and then watch them throw good food out." A single parent with three children to feed, she has struggled with providing for her family for over ten years.

The future looked bright for her when she married at 19. Her husband had a good business head and during most of their marriage he owned a successful clothing boutique. Debra, just a year out of high school, quit her job as a receptionist and stayed home with the children, who arrived in quick succession.

She had received no encouragement following high school to go on to post-secondary education. Her widowed father was just beginning his second marriage and, preoccupied with pleasing his new wife, he agreed with her that Debra, at 18, was capable of moving out on her own and supporting herself. She would no doubt find a husband in short order. "I was kicked out," Debra says with some bitterness. But ties with the rest of the family remained strong. When her marriage failed nine years later, Debra moved in with her brother and received financial help from all her siblings during the first year of her separation.

After a year's wait Debra and the children were able to move into public housing where the rent for a three-bedroom apartment is now being covered by the welfare department. She also receives $350 a month in financial assistance for food, clothing, and household essentials for her family of four and has no problem describing exactly where the local food bank is located. Five months ago her apartment and all her belongings (uninsured) were destroyed by fire. She and the three children now live temporarily in one room in an emergency shelter until they can get back into public housing.

When I met Debra at Tim Horton's, her face was showing the impact of this latest setback in her life. She has little animation, and a weary look of resignation speaks volumes. While she used to work as a receptionist before marriage, she now looks for work she can do at night so her eldest daughter can babysit. She and her children live in a different world now from the one they lived in for nine years.

Barbara Murphy

Bonnie, another single parent, was even younger than Debra when she married. At 18, six months out of school, she married her high school sweetheart. "My parents were not there to advise me," she recalls. "They had moved out of town a year earlier and I had chosen not to move from the high school where all my friends were." And perhaps she wouldn't have listened. She was in love with someone she planned to be with for the rest of her life. Four years later they separated and, when I met Bonnie, she was getting a divorce on the Internet.

During their marriage her young husband had difficulty holding a job; a developing drug dependence was part of the problem. Bonnie brought in an income of roughly $23,000 a year doing clerical work, a good part of her earnings going to a babysitter for her little girl born a year after they married. With this modest income, Bonnie was the principal breadwinner for the family.

After separating from her husband she could no longer afford the babysitter. She moved in with her father and applied for welfare. She now receives $500 a month for food, clothing, and household items and supplements her welfare income with work as a waitress. From $23,000 her annual income has dropped to $13,000.

But it is not her financial situation that has produced the greatest change in Bonnie's life. In fact, since her husband's earnings were so erratic, she has a new feeling of control over her finances now she is on her own. Instead, the most significant change is the total responsibility she has had to assume for her young child. With no one to share parenting tasks with, she often feels overwhelmed. Still young, only 24 now, she misses seeing friends and chafes at the restrictions of child care.

Single parents volunteered their stories for the interviews described in this chapter. Martha was one of them, calling to offer her help and leaving me her number and a cryptic telephone message: "I qualify. I've been there—the marriage, the separation, the divorce, the works." Now in her thirties, Martha looks back on her decisions when she was a high school student with more than a little cynicism. Experiencing some family and personal problems, she was determined to quit school at the end of grade ten. She did just that, at age 17. "I had in mind that some man would look after me," she admits.

Supporting herself with various part-time jobs as a retail sales clerk, she found her man within a year. Unfortunately, this solution to all her problems was short-lived. The steady income she had looked for in the man of her dreams proved to be an illusion. Not only was he unable to look after her financially as she had planned, he was also unable to look after the baby girl who arrived two years later. Without child care, the new addition to the family forced Martha to give up her retail job. Added to the unreliable financial support from her husband she was physically abused, the final straw that forced her to move out with her child and go on welfare.

Social assistance from the Ontario government totalled $990 a month; $890 went to her rent for a two-bedroom apartment. Even getting an apartment was difficult. Many landlords turned her down without a co-signer to a lease or a clear credit rating. Many also had minimum income requirements for a lease. Martha used her federal child tax credit of $100 a month to supplement the amount left over for food, clothing, diapers, and other items. She also paid the total cost of the divorce.

Although all this has taken its toll, Martha has taken steps to improve her employability for the future. While married and at home with her preschooler she completed her high school through correspondence courses (it took two and a half years). Ten years later, when her child was still in elementary school, she attended community college and trained as a developmental service worker with after-school child care provided by the welfare department. With her new training she worked with developmentally handicapped people for several years. More recently she is completing a B.A. in psychology with the help of student loans. She hopes to get a counselling job with her university degree.

barbara murphy

Asked how life changes after marriage break-up, Martha contends the greatest change is not financial but psychological. "Something happens to your self-esteem," she admits, "and you have to climb out of that." With the worst of the bad times behind her, Martha's life experiences seem to be propelling her into a new career where she can help others who suffer from the same problems of self-esteem she experienced herself.

In contrast to the new optimism in Martha's life, Shauna is a young single parent who so far sees no light at the end of the tunnel. A high school drop-out at 14, she spent two years living on the street, completely alienated from her family. At 16 she returned to finish school with financial help from an aunt. During those years—and in her earlier years at high school— she had good grades, but college or university were not options she could consider once ties with her immediate family were broken. And even with her new high school diploma, injuries from a car accident kept her from working and forced her to apply for a welfare disability allowance.

At 20 Shauna thought her luck was changing when she married a construction worker and began a family. The marriage lasted only four years, however, and she was left a year ago with a three-year-old boy, a baby on the way, and no child support.

On welfare again, Shauna has been able to get a two-bedroom apartment in public housing and has struggled to provide food, clothing, and diapers on $300 a month. She is a regular customer at the local food bank. While it doesn't carry the formula her doctor recommends for her infant, she finds she can exchange cans of food bank formula at the supermarket for the kind she needs.

As if her life were not chaotic enough, a new boyfriend moved in after her separation promising to help financially. He has since left, whereabouts unknown, and she is pregnant again.

Shauna's oldest child is now four years old. The energy and motivation she needs to provide him with some early

EATING THE WEDDING GIFTS

learning is not there. She rarely takes him out, her mobility restricted by her pregnancy and her past injuries. Her preoccupation with putting food on the table leaves little of herself for anything else. With no work experience and three preschoolers at home, Shauna cannot look to a brighter future for a while. One can only hope the same resourcefulness that got her off the street and back to high school ten years ago will help her back into the work force when her young preschoolers are older. At this point in her life, however, she is heartily fed up with the struggle.

Work experience is not one of Sylvie's problems. Another single parent with a story to tell, Sylvie has held a number of jobs since high school, but none of them has provided enough income to support more than one person. Faced now with supporting a young daughter on her own, she looks back over the past five years and wonders if the next five will be any better. "They certainly can't get any worse," she says. An attractive fair-haired woman in her thirties, she struggles constantly with money. Since her separation and divorce she has tried in vain to get child support from her ex-husband and is now anxiously trying to interpret a letter from Legal Aid that advises her they can no longer pay for her legal costs.

Raised in Quebec, Sylvie finished high school and took a sewing job immediately with a clothing manufacturing company in a small town. She was 17. She recalls there were no decisions to be made about continuing her education; her parents simply couldn't afford to help her and didn't encourage her to find other ways.

After supporting herself on her own wages for five years Sylvie married her steady boyfriend since high school and they moved to New Brunswick when he was stationed there with the army. Initially there were difficulties in the local job market with French her only language, but she eventually found work in a daycare centre. While she worked at the centre part-time, she took early childhood education training at night and got her certificate over two years.

Two years later a new posting for her husband to another province and a new baby on the way for Sylvie required some

barbara murphy

adjustment. In order to stay with her baby in their new home, Sylvie operated her own daycare centre at home which she ran for four or five years. "It supplemented my husband's income," she recalls, "but it didn't bring in a large amount of money." This fact only became a problem when her husband decided to leave.

She remembers the exact day five years ago. Her daughter was then three. Sylvie is now on welfare, living in subsidized housing. She does part-time cleaning while her daughter is at school but still finds there is never enough money for food or clothing. "A nutribar will get me through the day just fine," she says, "but I must feed my daughter properly." She makes regular visits to the food bank at the local community centre, especially from the middle of the month to the end.

Sylvie is currently enrolled in hotel and restaurant training at a community college. Staying up until one o'clock most nights to study, she has one more year of courses before she receives her diploma. She prays that will be the end of tight money, which is her main concern at the moment. What will she tell her daughter when it is her turn to graduate from high school? Sylvie doesn't hesitate for even a second: "Money is important in life. You will never realize it until you haven't got it. Get your education before you do anything else."

Another single parent, Christine, can date the break-up of her marriage from the day her husband struck her in the face and broke her nose. She left with her two children and within a short time moved to another province. The sudden break-up was the end of a dream she had planned at the end of high school, a dream of her own household where she would devote herself to being a wife and mother. It would be a symbol for her that she had "grown up." In the current climate of two working parents, Christine had her own vision of what married life would be like.

Interestingly, Christine had almost completed university when she married at 22. Always a student with good grades, she had entered university with a scholarship. But when the opportunity for a domestic life presented itself, she quit her studies and became a full-time wife. Over the next four years two children arrived and, with the arrival of the second, her carefully planned marriage became something she hadn't bargained for. Her young child was diagnosed with autism. Christine's life began to revolve around the child's special needs and the search for services that would help him. Looking back, she believes the strain took its toll on her husband, who became ill with depression and soon ran into financial difficulties.

Today Christine and her children live on welfare supplemented by her part-time work as a home support worker. While her husband's income was in the $45,000 to $50,000 range, the drop in income does not loom as large in her concerns as the fact she is now on her own advocating and constantly pushing for the special needs services her son requires. Life with a special needs child is filled with emotional upheavals and social difficulties. Her child, now six, is faced daily with not fitting in. "We can clear a playground in five minutes," Christine says with some of the humour that has seen her through these past five years.

Going on assistance and applying for public housing, according to Christine, are a "blow to your self-esteem." Although her part-time job as a home support worker is "nothing to get excited about" it helps to restore some of the value she used to feel about herself. In hindsight, she wishes she had completed her university—she may pick up the remaining credits some day—and, of course, she wishes she could share the burden of her autistic child with another parent. But events have overtaken her and Christine doesn't spend a lot of time thinking about what might have been. In a few years she plans to tell her daughter, now eight, not to be in a hurry to grow up and take on the responsibilities of a family.

Janice, a single parent for the past 20 years, realizes her life was on a downward spiral in the years following the break-up of her marriage, but she is determined she will never be caught short again. Now 45, Janice passes on this piece of advice to young women graduating from high school today:

barbara murphy

"Starting now, prepare for life as if you'll have to make it all on your own."

Janice left high school early, attracted at first by a job as a telephone operator and an opportunity for independence. Various retail jobs followed. Jobs that seemed adequate after high school were clearly never intended to provide enough income to support a family, yet that was the level of income she could count on when her marriage broke up. During the two years they were together her husband had earned good wages as a chef and she had contributed part-time earnings from her retail salesclerk job in a shoe store. "We were a typical two-income family," she recalls, "and we felt pretty good about our situation, especially with a baby on the way."

But the bubble burst when Janice's husband physically assaulted her. Frightened for herself and her infant, she moved into a shelter. "It was February 14th," she says with a shrug, "Valentine's Day." It was a rude jolt in her life but only the first. Applying for welfare while in the shelter, she was incredulous when she learned the financial assistance allowed for the two of them was intended to last a month, not a week!

Janice and her baby moved into a government-subsidized apartment after four months in the shelter. Within a year she was back at high school, taking her classes at a school that also provided daycare for her child. Books, food, clothing, and bus fare came out of her welfare cheque, and she turned to the food bank in the winter months when hydro bills were high. When she received her diploma (with honours) two years later she began to believe things could get better.

Finances were such a constant struggle, however, that she agreed to a trial reconciliation with her husband. It lasted four weeks, ending in another episode of violence. To make matters worse, Janice was pregnant again.

Today, 17 years after a restraining order finally kept her husband out of her life, she can list some accomplishments that give her pride. When her daughter reached school age, Janice completed a one-year training course offered by the Women's Credit Union as a preparation for careers in banking

EATING THE WEDDING GIFTS

and landed a job as customer service representative at a major bank. Five years later she entered community college and, after two years of study (with social assistance and her own part-time earnings), she received a social services diploma at the age of 36. She now works as a case coordinator providing social support services to people who are going through the same experiences she went through 20 years ago.

There is more than meets the eye in Rosa, a quiet, outwardly reticent woman who has been a single parent for over ten years. Behind her poise and reserve lies an amazing energy that has helped her to take on challenges and get a firm footing in the work world after her marriage fell apart. Though she still has serious concerns about being a partner in a marriage that failed, she is now an ideal role model for her daughter. Referring to the teenager she is bringing up on her own, she says: "I tell her, watch and learn."

Rosa, raised in a traditional Italian family, went into nursing college following high school. Disappointed that the daily routines and tasks of nurses left little time for personal rapport with patients, she gave up nursing after the first year of training. Not much more challenging was the job she then took with the government, doing clerical work which she describes as a continuous "paper chase."

Still working, Rosa married a construction worker when she was 23 and had her first child two years later. With their two incomes they paid a babysitter for child care and still had enough left over to live without financial stress. After their second child was born a year later, her husband's abusive behaviour began. Rosa's marriage ended abruptly after a frightening episode of violence, and she moved into an emergency shelter with her two children, one six months old and one 20 months old.

She recalls this period as the most devastating in her life. In the culture of her Italian community, marriages were expected to last, and women especially were expected to respect and hold on to their husbands. Rosa remembers vividly the low point she reached. She faced the mirror one day and

barbara murphy

pronounced herself a failure. Believing today that she was shouldering too much of the blame for her marriage break-up, she felt at the time that she could move ahead only after acknowledging she had hit bottom.

With help from the women's shelter she managed to get a two-bedroom apartment in subsidized housing and she went on social assistance. Like other single parents, she found out what it was like to live on a below-poverty-level welfare allowance; she struggled with baby food, clothing, and diaper needs for her two young children and many times found herself depressed. And then began her upward climb. While receiving welfare and subsidized child care she enrolled in university summer courses for a Bachelor of Social Work and finally into the regular program which she completed over the next four years. She worked in part-time social services jobs for a short period and then entered and completed the Master of Social Work program. All this was beyond her wildest dreams when she looked at herself in that mirror ten years earlier.

Today Rosa is a full-time social worker, but the struggle has been a long one. She is encouraging her daughter (who loves animals) to enrol in veterinarian school when she finishes high school or to get some other solid foundation in education that will keep her from hitting the rock bottom she herself hit when the unexpected happened.

Although hardship is said to build character, and even that is a question, most single parents would prefer to improve themselves some other way. Diane is another one who found what she could really accomplish only after her marriage broke up. Still, in retrospect, she wishes she had found out earlier.

Diane left high school at 14, was married at 15 (with her parents' legal permission but without their attendance at the ceremony), and had her first child at 16. Her marriage turned out to be a long ordeal of physical abuse which she failed to report. When her daughter was a teenager, the final episode took place. Her husband, angered when the teenager wouldn't turn over her babysitting earnings to him, exploded in a rage. Diane and her daughter were all too familiar with the signs that physical violence was about to erupt. "We ran," she says. "We ran, with only the clothes on our backs."

From a women's shelter Diane applied for welfare, and she and her daughter moved into an apartment two months later. The long struggle to make ends meet is a familiar one. With $900 a month from welfare for their total needs and $800 required for rent alone there was little left over for food. Diane, who had never held a job in her life, looked for work and found a full-time job with a telemarketing company that canvassed for used clothing for charity. Determined to make it work, she struggled to provide for her daughter and herself on minimum wage.

But she was soon out of a job when her employer declared bankruptcy. Answering an ad, she took cleaning work at a hotel not far from her home and was still able to meet the rent. Over the next year she was promoted to more senior duties, training new staff to clean the guest rooms and doing the cleaning in the less demanding common areas and offices herself. She was now working at a few dollars above the minimum wage. Her daughter, still at school, took a part-time job to help out. Things were definitely looking up.

Still working at the hotel, Diane enrolled in a community college training program for personal support workers, workers who help residents in retirement homes with their daily living. With a demanding timetable that involved attending classes on her days off from her hotel work, she gradually completed over three years the 12 modules that would normally take six months full time. She graduated with honours.

After landing a job as a personal support worker in a retirement home Diane quit her cleaning job at the hotel. Enjoying a better income, she recalls how completely dependent she was when she was married, totally reliant on someone else's earnings. She tells the story of arriving home recently to find a note on the door from her ex-husband, hoping to see her. Jarred by bitter memories for only a second, she tore up the note and moved on with her life.

barbara murphy

Sandy is another single parent who is familiar with the minimum-wage sector of the economy first-hand. Leaving high school at 16 to live with a boyfriend, she worked in a tele-marketing job for almost two years. By the time she was 18 both she and her boyfriend entered a rehabilitation program for treatment of drug abuse and, on completion, went their separate ways.

On her own Sandy needed welfare assistance briefly but soon landed a job as a waitress and moved from the YWCA into her own room. She was completely rehabilitated and proud of these first steps, living on her own two years before she met someone new and married at 21.

Finding subsidized housing, she and her husband combined their incomes from two minimum-wage jobs until their baby arrived a year later. Sandy began to work at home, doing piecework and caring for her child and, with their subsidized rent adjusted to their changed income, they managed to support themselves.

The marriage lasted nine years. When her husband left, Sandy went back to work as a waitress, but this time hers was the only income and she now had a child to support. She and her little boy moved in with the parents she was so anxious to leave at 16, and she pays room and board. Even with a reasonable room and board arrangement with her parents, Sandy has had to look for part-time work in addition to her full-time job. After a week of full-time work as a waitress, she spends the weekends working at a bakery.

Still, Sandy is proud of staying off welfare but, for that accomplishment, she works seven days a week. She has very little advice to offer today's young high school students. "I made some wrong decisions," she admits, "but I have to live with them." Not inclined to heed advice herself when she was in her teens, she believes whatever she may advise would fall on deaf ears. She is inclined to let her experiences of the past 15 years speak for themselves.

A single parent whose world has changed recently, Jennifer is still adjusting. Over twenty years ago when she was

EATING THE WEDDING GIFTS

19 she started university, then dropped out, and held a series of customer service jobs over the next few years with trust and investment firms. There seemed to be no serious repercussions to her decision to quit university, especially when a few years later she married a man with a comfortable income in the high tech sector.

After marriage Jennifer continued with sales work in the investment business until her first child was born. Suddenly with a downturn in the high tech business, she and her husband found themselves in financial difficulties for the first time. They moved to another province where her husband took a new job, and Jennifer had to get work in the evenings at a courier call centre so she could care for her child during the day. Another child arrived. It was the worst possible time for her husband's career to falter but, within a short time, he was forced to look for work again back in their home province.

Through these difficult years their marriage suffered and finally fell apart completely. Jennifer was left with two school-age children, eight and eleven. She found secretarial work, courier call-taking work again, then a job coordinating special events, and she received financial support from her husband. But it was a struggle. "The problem was I never established a career path," Jennifer says. "Because things were going well at first, I never thought about it. But I would advise young people to do it before they have children." She likes to compare her own situation to the planning steps she was taught in her recent job as an events coordinator. "Besides planning time lines, goals, and budget," she recalls, "you have to think about and plan for What if ...?"

Teresa, a recent single parent, is raising two children on her own without the job training or experience she had promised herself when she was younger. Her former husband's ethnic background was the deciding factor in their married life—wives were expected to stay home to care for a working husband and their children. Teresa had planned to train as a dental nurse, but gave up her ambition when she married at 19.

barbara murphy

Staying home, she felt confined. After two children arrived, she began to take correspondence courses. She could learn dental theory at home; the practical part would have to wait. In the meantime they lived comfortably on her husband's public service income.

———— . ————

Teresa's marriage broke up when her second child was two years old. She still dreams of finishing her dental nurse training, but she is now on welfare, hoping a subsidized child care space will become available. Raising two children on her own, she is totally preoccupied with stretching money, buying used clothing, and going regularly to the food bank. She knows now she sacrificed several years of her life by trying to please the demands of her husband. "I'm not a good one to give advice," she admits, "but a woman should find a guy who is interested in her life and her career as well as his."

Interviews with single parents are not characterized by confidences drawn out of reluctant young women who would really prefer to withhold their feelings about a serious setback in their lives. On the contrary, most interviews are like a dam bursting. There is bitterness, insight into the underlying dynamic of events, and regret—they are comfortable with a whole gamut of feelings and want to share them.

At a critical point in the course of their lives—the completion of high school—the choices made by these single parents were influenced by a number of factors. Some were beyond their control. In the case of Shauna and Sylvie, financial considerations narrowed their options. Uncontrollable events also affected Debra, who was forced out on her own when her father remarried. But in most cases personal motivation and personalities in general were the major influences on their decisions not to complete some form of higher education.

Christine dropped out of university to fulfill her dream of domesticity; Rosa dropped out of nursing hoping to find a more challenging, people-oriented type of career; Martha's goal was marriage and a man to look after her; Janice was attracted by the (short-term) financial independence she would have as a telephone operator with Bell; and Bonnie, alone and 18 after her parents moved away, married to create a home for herself.

Almost all these single parents concede that their choices at the time were not conscious decisions made with a view to how they might affect the rest of their lives. (Diane, especially, made a decision to marry at 15, an age that society does not consider adult either legally or in a broader social sense involving judgment.) Also missing were close advisers who could impress on them the importance of conscious decisions at this important stage of their lives. For many, such long-term decisions came after the havoc of marriage break-up and raising children in poverty, giving further evidence that the personal strengths were there at the outset but received too little emphasis and too little support.

Barbara Murphy

Chapter 6

HIGHER-INCOME SINGLE PARENTS, THEIR STORIES

The psychological and emotional fall-out at the end of a marriage is well known to therapists, doctors, and those involved in crisis intervention. Some single parents report stress-related illnesses following divorce; others suffer from depression. Repairing the damage to feelings of self-worth also requires time and the emotional support of others. It would be a serious misconception to believe anyone sails through the experience without any scars.

Heartbreak and depression are not reserved for single parents left with raising children in poverty. Women with more than adequate incomes are also hurt personally by marriage break-up. It makes sense, however, that personal damage is healed sooner when a single parent is not faced with a devastating loss of control over the survival needs of her children and herself. Control is an essential ingredient in feelings of self-esteem; without it, individuals are trapped by the chance events of life and eventually give up the goal of breaking free.

Women who can fall back on better-paying jobs report that stresses begin to disappear as they discover they can provide for their families and once more take control of their lives. Most of these women have stories with happier endings.

Caroline, a single parent and sole provider of her family, is one. Raised in a large family of six children, she recalls that she worked at many different jobs during her adolescent years. When she finished high school in a town without a university she knew her parents' financial situation would not allow her to attend university away from home, even though she had done well in school. At that critical stage in her life her choices were either some other form of post-secondary education or a job. In the end the choice was not difficult. With her own first-hand experience during her teens she knew all too well the nature of minimum wage work. She was determined to prepare herself for something more challenging. Lining up some part-time jobs to see her through, she enrolled in business administration at the local community college.

Two years later, with her business administration diploma on her resumé, Caroline landed a good job in a property management firm. Within a year she was made an area manager. Still only 20, she met and married a university lecturer, and they had 12 years of what she now calls "normal life." They lived comfortably, raising three children with their combined earnings of $85,000 a year. But their comfortable marriage suddenly came to an end when her husband physically assaulted her. Frightened and shattered by this sudden change in her husband's personality, Caroline moved out with the children.

Her salary of $43,000 allowed her to get after-school child care and continue to work. But working through her own emotional adjustment while taking on the role of family breadwinner made for some difficult times. "It was no picnic," Caroline recalls. Partly due to stress, she became ill for a short period and the family income was reduced to her unemployment insurance entitlement. But it was a temporary setback. With her health back to normal, she has returned to her regular job as area manager and has enrolled in part-time studies at university, determined to move ahead.

As a result of her own experience with marriage Caroline is raising her daughters to prepare for a life of financial

Barbara Murphy

independence. She has insisted each of them enroll in the academic stream in high school. Despite her well-paid job, the family income is only half what it was when she was married, but it has made the difference in what she can provide for them. Her oldest daughter finished high school in Ontario last year and, in contrast to Caroline who could not attend university away from home because of her family's financial situation, now attends university in another province. She is financing her education with scholarships and her own earnings, with some help from her mother. "I'm immensely proud of what she has done on her own," Caroline says. She is determined her daughters will stand on their own two feet, prepared for a life of financial independence no matter what curves are thrown their way.

Tanya is the heroine of quite a different kind of success story. She was raised in an educated family in Bosnia with the clear expectation that she would go on to university after high school. Although the decision seemed predetermined, the years at university suited her perfectly. She had been a constant reader right from childhood and any kind of learning satisfied her insatiable curiosity.

After graduating with a B.A. in economics she was hired by a foreign trade firm in Bosnia. Within a few short years she rose to a managerial position that involved responsibility for the export and import of a variety of goods and for maintaining business relationships with her counterparts in many other countries. Her facility in English was another important asset in foreign trade. With the satisfaction of using most of her skills, Tanya loved her job. "Work gives me energy," she confesses.

She was 26 when she married a mechanical engineer who was taking his master's degree. Still enjoying her own career, Tanya supported them both, and when a baby arrived a year later she returned to work after maternity leave, placing her child in a daycare program. When her husband finished his graduate studies he took a new job and they enjoyed the financial comfort of two incomes. But the marriage lasted only four years when her husband made a decision to leave.

In the years following separation and divorce Tanya continued to provide for her growing child with her good salary. But there were still other challenges ahead. By the time her daughter was in her early teens, Bosnia was thrown into upheaval by war. Fearing for their lives, Tanya made arrangements to move out of the country, hoping to start a new life for herself and her daughter in Canada. Although there were expenses involved, her income allowed her to do what many other women in her country couldn't do on their own.

In Canada it took some time for her to secure the kind of well-paying job she had before the war. Earning less, it was difficult; she suffered two episodes of depression. But she refused to wait around for employers to recognize her foreign credentials and her work experience in economics. She took work in another field and continued to provide for her daughter and herself. Today Tanya looks back on the choices and decisions she made, knowing she was able to make them because of the confidence she gained through her education and the financial resources she was able to draw upon through her work. "I don't know why it is," she says, "but education somehow makes you feel you can do anything, even if it's entirely new." It's a message she wants to pass on to her daughter.

Natasha is another single parent who has few regrets about the choices she made when she was younger. Raised in Quebec, she recalls very little discussion on the subject of university; it was simply understood by her parents and herself that she would someday attend. When she finished CEGEP at 19, however, Natasha decided university could wait. She headed west.

During the next year she held every imaginable unskilled job in Vancouver and Banff—from dishwashing to waiting on tables—while living in communal housing arrangements with other young people doing the same. Looking for new experiences, she and two friends went on to Europe for several months, finding work where they could but, for the most part, living on their earnings of the previous year. University

barbara murphy

enrolment seemed to move farther and farther down the list of priorities. "What we must have put our parents through!" Natasha admits.

Back in Canada she headed west again and held a variety of jobs, including waitress, chambermaid, even cleaning up camp grounds for Parks Canada. But at 21, she recalls, she decided she had had enough of travelling, part-time jobs, and impermanence. She enrolled at a university in Alberta. With the help of student loans, she put herself through with a combination of part-time work and part-time study, graduating when she was 26 with a B.A. in psychology and sociology and starting a career in social work. A few years later she attended graduate school, completing the Master of Social Work program.

With a successful career underway, Natasha turned to new life experiences—marriage and motherhood. Her marriage lasted less than two years. On her own again but with new responsibilities, she set out to make a home for herself and her new baby. But her plans received a setback when she went through an unexpected period of depression. She remembers vividly the competing emotions. Mixed in with feelings of isolation and abandonment were feelings of anger. Although she received financial support from her ex-husband, she resented being the only parent on hand most of the time, carrying almost all the weight alone, planning for the child's future without help.

Today Natasha has resolved most of these problems. With her earnings she has purchased a townhouse. Still living alone with her child, she has worked out a co-parenting arrangement that is now working, a clearly defined sharing of responsibilities and decisions. "Child-rearing is the biggest job in the world," she says. "You have this little life you're responsible for." She has continued with her career, crediting it not only with her financial independence but with feelings of self-esteem that have been fully restored. "When that part of your life is going well," she says, "you feel together enough to raise a child."

EATING THE WEDDING GIFTS

Many women with university degrees claim the whole university experience gave them new personal strengths they never knew they had, in addition to the academic skills they originally signed up for. Helen, a single parent with one child, admits she was a timid, anxious-to-please teenager whose only brave show of defiance was to insist she would go into dentistry when her parents began to make plans for her to study theology after high school. The choice of taking some form of higher education was never in question—it was simply which field to enter.

Today Helen has no regrets about her choice. She came out of university with an honours degree in dentistry and a new feeling of control that had been missing in her life. Even before graduation she had lined up a good government job in public health, specializing in children's dental needs. Within a year or two, she moved on, heading up a private clinic which also served children, and ending up buying the clinic herself.

When she married a few years later she and her husband, a physicist, started up a lab for the manufacture of dental alloy. She gave up her active role in the child dental clinic at her husband's insistence when their first baby arrived two years later but continued to work in the lab. They manufactured a highly successful product until they separated within a few short years.

It was not an amicable separation. With her new personal strengths and his need to dominate she had been the first to see the marriage was not working. She took the initiative in separation and divorce proceedings, but lost both her share of the dental alloy business and any possessions they had accumulated during their marriage.

Instead of returning to her job as full-time director of her own children's clinic, however, Helen's world took a sudden shift in direction. From her role as anxious-to-please teenager ten years earlier she was now the one her family turned to for help. Her younger sister was embroiled in many personal problems, including early steps toward drug abuse and difficulty in getting work, and Helen was urged to take her under her wing.

barbara murphy

Now, supporting her two-year-old child on her own for the first time, she also began to sort out her younger sister's life. She sold her private dental clinic and, without any previous experience in the garment business, she bought a clothing manufacturing business where she hoped her sister could learn a skill, acquire the discipline of regular work hours, and earn a wage.

It worked. Over the past 15 years her sister has moved into every position in the business and is now responsible for most of the design, manufacturing, and marketing. For her part, Helen is looking for a new challenge. She may go back and upgrade her professional qualifications or she may try lab work again. She has the financial resources to do either. In the meantime she is channeling her own daughter, now 17, into science courses at high school that will prepare her for a career in dentistry if she should make that choice.

Erin, another single parent, made some choices after high school that convinced her she could not imagine a lifetime of work that failed to challenge her brain and her creative skills. But this revelation took place only after almost two years of trying out what she calls low-end jobs. It was her mother, concerned about the growing rates of marriage break-up, who urged her to think about a career that would always provide her with financial independence.

Still not fully committed to a particular field, Erin began studies in general arts at a university in Alberta. Then, following a summer of field work as a guide in a provincial park, she became interested in history and began to major in that subject. She completed her undergraduate degree by the time she was 20 and decided to move east. With earnings over the next year and student loans she enrolled in a graduate degree program, taking her M.A. in international studies.

Marriage was next on the agenda. Erin and her husband, both working (Erin with a communications job), brought in a good income and within three years a daughter arrived. With her new baby she began to work at home, consulting and freelance writing, finding a special niche in speech writing.

EATING THE WEDDING GIFTS

But her marriage was deteriorating with continuous arguments that made for an unhappy household. She held things
together until her daughter began school, then she and her
husband separated.

Erin struggled through major changes, moving from a
country home to the city, taking on full responsibility for her
daughter, and expanding her consulting business into full-
time work, but financial considerations were never her major
concern. She and her daughter now live comfortably and
without some of the earlier tensions of her married years.

Having a daughter of her own, Erin has no hesitation in
choosing appropriate advice for young women leaving high
school. "Think ahead about how you would look after your-
self on your own," she advises. "The world is changing—
women plan careers now and think about marriage and children later."

Nicole, with a son and a daughter, recalls that she took a
considerable time to adjust when her marriage broke up.
Taken by surprise, she wonders now if she could have given
the children more emotional support than she did. She
believes that her father, stepping into the gap when her husband left, played an important role in helping the children
through a difficult time. When she finally recovered her emotional balance she was able to take over again, but she feels
she owes the remarkable adjustment on the part of the children to her father.

She and her father had not always been so understanding
of each other. After her mother died when Nicole was only 12,
she battled with him throughout her teenage years as if, she
now believes, she blamed him for her mother's death. He set
clear standards for Nicole and her younger sister and was usually inflexible about the rules he imposed for their social life
and their schooling.

Nicole recalls that for her part she was anxious to go to
university but resented that he had laid out that path for her on
his own. "In my mind he couldn't do anything right, even if it
was what I wanted," she says today. "In retrospect, he was

barbara murphy

trying to be two parents rolled into one. It makes it more understandable." She completed a Bachelor of Arts program (as did her sister) and went on to graduate studies in social work, finishing when she was 23.

Showing some leadership in her early social services jobs, Nicole moved into a senior position relatively quickly. About this time she married a lawyer who was also in his twenties. Over the next years she managed to juggle her social work career and the raising of two children and enjoyed the challenge of both parts of her life. The family lived comfortably on two professional incomes. Although there was still some strain between her father and herself, she believes he was very proud of her.

When her husband left unexpectedly she thought she would never recover, but somehow her social work experience helped her understand the stress she was under. She continued to work, arranged to hold onto the family home, and tried to keep things as stable as possible for the children. "I couldn't have done any of those things without my income," she claims, "and certainly not without the emotional support from my father, which came out of the blue."

What would she tell young women finishing high school? "Don't stop your education right there," Nicole says. "Don't even think about it. Where would the children and I be without my good job? They'll be heading to university themselves in a few years and I want to be in a position to help them."

Post-secondary education, especially university, can open the way for women to a lifetime of economic independence regardless of marriage break-up. The level of economic independence can be considerably lowered, however, if women graduates have long interruptions to their careers after marriage. In fact, men also fall behind in their careers during extended absences from the labour force, but women are more likely than men to make such a choice. At the very least labour force dropouts with post-secondary education must start again at the entry level. Wendy, a single parent interviewed for this study, believes dropping out of the full-time work force made a substantial impact on her after-divorce income.

Finished high school at 18, Wendy worked for a year as a bank teller, and then enrolled in university, financing her studies with part-time work. A year short of graduation she married, but continued until she had her degree. Both Wendy and her husband, who had already completed his MBA, agreed to focus on his career. His income, they calculated, would be sufficient to support the family as two children arrived within the next two years. Wendy took a part-time job in the evenings, leaving her days free to care for the children.

They enjoyed what seemed to be a good marriage for 13 years when it ended abruptly shortly after the birth of their third child. Wendy's husband had found someone else. She remembers as if it was yesterday the day she and the three children moved out of the house into a rented townhouse. She was still in the part-time evening job she had held for over ten years. Now on her own, however, her salary seemed woefully inadequate.

Her husband provided spousal and child support for five years, but payments stopped, and Wendy has accrued substantial legal costs trying to get support started again, especially for one child, 12 years old, still at home. In the meantime, she has not been successful in getting a full-time job that raises her income to the level of other university graduates. The drop in her standard of living has been unexpected and difficult for her to accept. She relies on considerable financial help from her family.

Balancing career and children is not easy. In Wendy's case, from the time she interrupted her career until the present she has lost ground in the job market that may take a while to regain. Now 20 years since the year of her graduation, she believes it may be more worthwhile to return to university for a graduate degree to update her skills and make herself more competitive.

—·—

barbara murphy

Single parents with university degrees have a different experience after marriage break-up than do those with only high school education. There are both emotional and financial differences. While they still suffer the emotional consequences of a failed personal relationship, their periods of depression are relatively brief, can be sidetracked more readily by the demands of their careers, and are totally free of the demoralizing effects of trips to the food bank.

It is not surprising that we hear less of the aftermath of their divorces than of those of less educated single parents. For one thing, marriage break-up is associated with educational levels. Women with university degrees are only one-third as likely to experience marital dissolution as other women.[76]

We can only speculate why this is so. If university comes before marriage, three or four years may make a difference in how well partners are chosen. Perhaps those years add a dimension to judgment that is missing in the early 20s. Perhaps with the added maturity of a few years both men and women are more inclined to consider long-term goals than their younger counterparts, long-term goals that include a stronger desire for stability than the search for new experiences.

Perhaps, too, the marriages of women with degrees have fewer financial problems and, to the extent that financial matters contribute to the deterioration of a marriage, their marriages may be less affected. Many studies have documented the link between financial difficulties and broken marriages. Although these may be reasons for lower divorce rates among women with higher education, the smaller numbers that do divorce appear to have less devastating experiences than those with only high school diplomas.

Salaries are an important variable. The case histories of six university-educated single parents interviewed illustrate that incomes from their own work made the largest difference. Caroline can help a daughter at university away from home; Helen's salary as a dentist allowed her to raise her daughter comfortably after divorce and come to the rescue of her sister; Erin's consulting income allowed her to plan her separation on her own timetable; and Nicole was able to hang on to the family home which made transition easier for the children.

Other single parents found their university experience and their good jobs gave them the confidence to take on challenges that were not necessarily related to their education or career. Tanya left Bosnia with her daughter with not only the financial resources to do it but the feeling she could meet any challenges in a new country successfully. Helen went into the manufacture of clothes with no experience in that field but a considerable amount of faith in her own management abilities after running a clinic. Even Wendy, whose situation has been anything but financially comfortable following her divorce, can see herself back at school and eventually back at a job more in line with her education.

All these single parents would have preferred a marriage that lasted longer. But they have picked up the pieces and moved on. What they have in common is a sense that they are now coping well and can turn their attention from themselves to the children they are responsible for.

Barbara Murphy

Chapter 7

COMPETING THEORIES OF SINGLE-PARENT POVERTY

Higher education can spell the difference for a single parent between raising her children with sufficient financial resources and raising them in poverty. But is the idea of education as the major, if not the only, cause of poverty for young single parents too simple? Based on almost universal agreement that social problems have multiple causes, it is worthwhile exploring other influences identified by social researchers, including some that enjoy popular appeal in an era of public spending restraint.

Linking higher education with economic well-being falls under the heading of structural arguments. Given that the economic system rewards educated workers with higher salaries and relegates unskilled workers to the bottom of the wage scale, the resulting inequities can be seen to be embedded in a nation's economic structure. In fact, the situation is not nation-specific, but characterizes the structure of the international economy. Social scientists have formalized the inequitable split of earners in all European and North American countries by proposing the idea of a dual labour market. This structural argument associating poverty with lack of education is also valid for Canada and, as statistics in

Chapter 3 illustrate, it can explain the high incidence of poverty among single parents, over 90 percent of whom are currently without university degrees.

Other theories enjoy popularity, however, arguments that the social and economic structure plays no part at all in the creation of poverty. These theories lie at the far end of the spectrum from pure structural theories. They see the causes of poverty as personal failure and the solution to poverty as the correction of the character deficiencies of the poor rather than the improvement of wage minimums or welfare allowances. This position underlies so-called welfare reform in many countries, including Canada, during the 1990s. It is somewhat reminiscent of Poor Law reforms of the early 19th century when local ratepayers in England pressed for more restrictive criteria for the granting of assistance—usually a loaf of bread per month—to vagrants and other unemployed individuals. Arguing that the poor were lazy and shiftless and were becoming even more so with every free loaf of bread they were given, the rules were changed and the poor could receive food only if they lived and worked in a workhouse.

The late 20th century witnessed a revival of this approach to poverty in both Europe and North America. Especially in the U.S., researchers began to attribute rising poverty rates to character deficiencies of the poor themselves.[77] These theories received less attention by academic writers in Canada[78] but were enthusiastically embraced by a few provincial governments, notably Alberta and Ontario, who set about to "reform" their welfare policies on the premise that people on the welfare rolls were quite capable of holding a job but really preferred not to.

The reform of welfare was also based on the belief that increased welfare spending over three decades had, if anything, made these very character deficiencies of the poor even worse. "Generous" allowances had acted as disincentives to work and, in the case of single parents, had actually been the cause of increasing marriage breakdown by making it easier for women to leave their husbands. Or if the husband was the one to go, higher levels of social assistance made him more comfortable about leaving his wife and children without an income. Once on welfare, according to the argument, the poor become overly dependent, lose the drive to be self-reliant, and remain for long periods on the welfare rolls.

A variation of the claim that poverty is caused by individual characteristics of the poor is the theory that the poor are not only lazy and shiftless but, in fact, have their own value system, one that is at odds with the values of mainstream society. A value system with no emphasis on the work ethic or sense of self-reliance, it has been argued, becomes part of a subculture embraced by the poor that is reinforced from generation to generation, creating a cycle of poverty. Given the tenacity of the subculture, breaking out of the cycle becomes almost impossible. With this fatalistic view of poverty, it becomes easier for social scientists and policymakers to argue that there is no point in throwing more money at it.

Although the idea of an undeserving class of welfare recipients was attractive to many in the general public, many of the "welfare reform" claims about the abuse of the system by people who should be out working were never supported with evidence. It was true the number of single parents had increased. The basic premise of generous allowances as the cause, however, failed to hold up. Little attention was given by welfare reformers (and the media and the general public) to the fact that since the 1970s, welfare allowances in all parts of Canada had declined in real value because they were never adjusted to inflation. Yet the number of single parents continued to grow. Were more and more wives leaving their husbands, lured by the mistaken impression that allowances were going up rather than down? And how was it possible to trace increased marriage breakdown to higher welfare allowances that made husbands feel comfortable about leaving when the reality was that the capacity of the welfare system to give anyone comfort was declining?

In attributing unrealistic incentives to the welfare system, critics were overlooking other obvious causes. Most research on marriage breakdown in Canada has tied its recent increase to more liberalized access to divorce provided in the new legislation of 1968 and 1985. The century-long trend toward increased marriage breakdown can be attributed to even broader social change, as described in Chapter 1, primarily more relaxed attitudes about the sanctity of marriage and the increased economic independence of women which has made the dissolution of a bad marriage a more viable alternative than it was in the past.

Evidence has also been sketchy in making a connection between long periods on welfare and increasing dependency. The Economic Council of Canada, after an exhaustive study of the transition of Canadians into and out of poverty, concludes that their findings cannot confirm that the longer on welfare the more likely welfare recipients are to lose their motivation to be economically independent. Another range of factors explains why some remain dependent. In the case of the mentally and physically disabled and single parents with young children, the Council cautions, "it is not appropriate to argue that they remain poor simply because they have lost the habits and attributes of self-reliance."[79]

The argument that the poor have a different value system than the rest of society is also short on evidence. An American study of over 3,000 residents in poor, segregated neighbourhoods in the inner city of Chicago has shown quite the opposite to be true. Questions asked of residents covered opportunity and mobility, work experiences and opinions about work, education and expectations for their children, social class, and finances. Over 78 percent of respondents preferred a job to any form of government assistance; three-quarters believed that plain hard work was important in getting ahead in life. "What is clear from our research," the study concludes, "is that the residents share values that cut across [other income] groups in the United States."[80]

A study of poverty in Canadian cities, especially its concentration in neighbourhoods, uses Census data rather than interviews to determine if a different set of cultural habits, lifestyles, and values exists for the poor.[81] Looking for indications of this "culture" of poverty, it traces the intergenerational mobility of various ethnic groups along both educational and occupational dimensions. The study concludes that in some cases, especially the case of visible minorities, poverty may nurture a distinct culture in which the desire for upward social mobility and improvement in economic status is absent. The findings, according to the study, illustrate that a "culture" of poverty is an *outcome* of poverty, not its original cause, and is not a universal finding. Still, to the extent that its main characteristics are fatalism and dependence, it can perpetuate poverty in succeeding generations and can become a *cause* over time for some groups.

Debate about the cause of poverty in general is sometimes reduced to two opposing views which, appropriately or not, are also applied to the poverty of single parents. If causes are found either in society's structure or in the individual characteristics of some of its members, an argument about the importance of young women's personal decisions at the end of high school falls somewhere in the middle. The commonly held theory that social class (i.e., the income and occupation of a family) influences such decisions, especially as they relate to pursuing a university education, provides a structural perspective. I have argued otherwise in Chapter 2, or at least that the influence of social class is modest. One has only to look at the university enrolment and graduation figures of first-generation Canadians to make the point.

The influence of social class is not only modest, it is overshadowed by parental expectations (no matter what the social class), the relative importance of personal freedom to young people in general at this stage of the life cycle, and the appeal of marriage and motherhood to young women in particular. Making the choice of early marriage with its 60-40 chance of success can lead to poverty for these same young women. The argument, then, has emphasized personal choice while acknowledging the strong tendency of the economic structure to assign women to low-wage jobs before, during, and after marriage. In other words, it acknowledges that there have been some inroads (Canadian university statistics have shown) into the longstanding relationship between social class and university enrolment, but very little progress in loosening the tendency of Canada's economic structure to place men and women inequitably within it.

—— • ——

While debate about the cause of poverty centres on a dual labour market, the personal deficiencies of the poor, or a flawed value system, it is easy to overlook a simpler explanation, especially in relation to the poverty of separated or divorced single parents. Two important contributions are made by the divorce process itself. They are attractive as causes because they are not without solution.

The first contribution made by the divorce process is the longstanding practice of assigning sole (rather than joint) custody of children in the majority of divorce settlements and, in making sole custody awards, assigning custody to the mother. In most cases the mother will come out of divorce proceedings (that end up in court) with responsibility for the care of the children of the marriage. She will also have care of the children in most of the informal arrangements that never reach court. Here lies the real root of her poverty. She becomes poor because she has additional mouths to feed, a greater number of bedrooms to rent, and more of the other necessities of life to provide than she would have if she were only providing for herself.

The historical tendency for the courts to assign sole custody of children to the mother has been well-documented. In the mid-1980s roughly 73 percent of children were placed in the custody of their mother, 15 percent in the custody of their father, and one percent in joint custody.[82] By 2002 awards of sole custody to either parent had dropped dramatically from 88 percent to 58 percent as a result of a remarkable growth in joint custody awards (from one percent to 42 percent in just 16

barbara murphy

years).[83] Within this reduced proportion of sole custody awards, however, the custody of children is assigned to the mother in 84 percent of cases. And, for the most part, residency is still with the mother in joint custody cases.

These figures refer only to agreements reached in court, but the percentage of awards to the mother is even larger in reality. The vast majority of divorces are granted without a formal court hearing. Taking into account all children, whether in formal or informal divorce agreements, and looking specifically at residency, a 1998 longitudinal study of children after separation showed that 86 percent lived with their mother, 7 percent lived with their father, and 6 percent lived under shared custody, living equal time with each parent.[84]

With female earnings in Canada still only 64 percent of male earnings, it seems logical to ask why the majority of divorce settlements add the financial burden of children to the parent with the least potential to provide for them. Of course, the intention is that the other partner will help out financially, but this is not always the case (more on this situation later).

How can we explain this logic? When decisions are made by court order, a range of factors are taken into consideration. Financial ability is only one of them. Over the past 30 years the paramount consideration in such cases has been the child's best interests. It is difficult to change traditional views, however, of what is best for the child. As a result, court decisions tend to move along at the pace of slowly changing attitudes. Before 1976 courts used the so-called "tender years doctrine" in awarding custody, an approach that reflects a judgment of the 1930s that "the general rule is that the mother, other things being equal, is entitled to the custody and care of a child during what is called the period of nurture, namely, until it attains about seven years of age, the time during which it needs the care of the mother more than that of the father."[85]

The tender years doctrine has been used in many Canadian decisions over the years. A Supreme Court of Canada decision in 1976, however, rejected it. It was informally replaced with the "primary caregiver" argument that the partner providing primary care to the child before separation should be awarded custody. This argument emphasized the importance of stability, consistency, and continuity of care for children at a time of dramatic change in their lives. The result was that this criterion naturally identified the mother in the primary caregiver role. Regardless of these earlier approaches, Canadian divorce legislation now stipulates that the court is to take into consideration only the best interests of the child. But there remains some controversy about whether the "tender years" and "primary caregiver" principles are indeed dead.

Controversy about the tenacity of old principles in court orders has unfortunately split along gender lines. Both men's groups and women's groups have been vocal on recent issues related to proposed changes to the Divorce Act. Men's groups have claimed that the "tender years" doctrine still lingers in court decisions about child custody, creating a gender bias in the justice system. Women's groups have claimed that the changes in legislation proposed by their male counterparts will seriously jeopardize the safety of women who have left marriages because of violence. In cases not involving violence, they still argue in favour of the primary caregiver principle. Taking a step back from the controversy, which for the most part centres on court settlements, one can see some merit in supporting changes that would relieve some of the financial burden on women, especially when that financial burden locks their families in poverty.

With joint custody awards on the increase, this type of award could be the most fruitful in the search for a solution to the poverty of single-parent families. In cases where the joint custody award is "joint custody with primary residency" (i.e., primary residency with the mother)—and indeed this is the situation in over 90 percent of such awards[86]—there is room for spreading the care of the children more equitably without disturbing any agreement about residency. Daytime hours five days a week could be the responsibility of the father, who would not only be responsible for taking children to and from paid child care but would also be responsible for paying the

barbara murphy

child care bill. Relieved of the burden of providing the care of the children herself or of paying someone else to care for them, the mother could more successfully make ends meet by pursuing a career that is otherwise a difficult prospect when she has child care responsibilities. As a proposed solution, it has the added advantage of daily contact between children and their father after separation when, most will agree and certainly the Divorce Act stipulates, it is in the best interests of the child to have maximum contact with both parents.

While women's and men's groups in Canada have conflicting views of the benefits of joint custody, some interesting studies have emerged in the U.S. where joint custody awards gained popularity earlier than in Canada. One national study in the 1990s found that states with high levels (over 30 percent) of joint custody awards showed significantly greater declines in divorce rates in the following five years compared with other states.[87] Another study found that fathers with joint custody pay more child support than in cases where mothers have sole custody. In addition, fathers with joint custody see their children more often and have more overnight visits. The study concludes that this finding of more frequent contact supports the argument, increasingly voiced by child advocates, that joint custody may allow the lives of children after divorce to resemble more closely their lives before divorce or the lives of their peers in two-parent households.[88]

With its tendency to award custody of children to the mother, it is clear the divorce process itself contributes to the poverty of single-parent families. A change to this practice appears to be on the way, and who knows to what extent recent declines in the Canadian divorce rate can be attributed to new shared custody arrangements. Another piece of the divorce process, on the other hand, is showing less change. Child support continues to be a major problem for many female single parents who have been assigned custody with the expectation of financial assistance from the non-resident father.

EATING THE WEDDING GIFTS

Estimates of the extent of compliance with child support orders vary. Some orders are paid in full, some in part, and some are in arrears. Statistics Canada now collects data on the enforcement of support payments directly from provincial maintenance enforcement programs which, it is estimated, handle less than one-half of all support orders and agreements in Canada. Data is collected for both child and spousal support, making up most of support orders registered, and a smaller number relating to spouse-only support.[89]

In March, 2003, the Maintenance Enforcement Survey reported a range of 21 percent (Quebec) to 51 percent (P.E.I.) of support payments in arrears in six provinces surveyed. Reflecting the average, Ontario and B.C. reported roughly 40 percent of cases in arrears. These included payments not made in the month they were due or payments made on time but not in the full amount due. A fifth to a half of cases in arrears involved payments not made in over a year or never made at all.

Using another measure, the federal survey found that provincial enforcement programs failed to collect up to 30 per cent of support dollars due in 2003. This gap between what is collected and what is due has a huge impact on single parents in Canada by leaving them millions of unpaid dollars short for food, shelter, clothing, and other necessities for their families. Quebec, for example, collected 89 percent of the $406 million due, leaving single parents $45 million short for living expenses. In B.C. single parents were also left $45 million short; in Saskatchewan, $6 million short. Ontario, whose figures were not available for the 2002-3 federal survey, released its own figures later in 2003 through the publication of the provincial auditor's report. In all, 136,000 cases were in arrears, leaving single parents $1.3 billion short.[90] The total support dollars not collected in only five provinces, therefore, amounted to $1.4 billion.

Unlike the shift in custody awards, which could gradually improve the financial situation of female single parents, the history of child support arrears offers little hope. Since data collection began four years ago, provincial success rates have

barbara murphy

remained roughly the same. Trying to locate where the problem lies is made more difficult by media charges of "deadbeat dads." A federal research study into arrears concluded that the perception that most fathers in Canada deliberately refuse to make court-ordered support payments is not accurate. The reality, according to the study, is that many fathers are broke or only unintentionally in arrears.[91] Similarly, the 2003 Maintenance Enforcement Survey reported that arrears can occur for a variety of reasons such as stays of enforcement proceedings, prolonged periods of social assistance, unemployment, disability, or incarceration.[92] Seasonal workers can also fall behind in payments when they are not working, and often they cannot afford to go back to court to seek a variance to the court-ordered support.

Whatever the reasons, women left with the care of children are often saddled with the total expense of that care without financial help from the children's father. Recalling that the majority of female single parents are poor, the absence or irregularity of child support payments contributes significantly to their poverty. Over 80 percent of poor single parents do not receive child or spousal support.[93] Adding together the frequent assignment of custody or residency to mothers and the frequent non-compliance with child support orders by fathers for whatever reason, the process and practices of going through a divorce can make a significant contribution to the poverty of female single parents.

— • —

A review of the causes of poverty requires a brief examination of the role of out-of-wedlock births to teenagers and the tendency over the past two decades for these young mothers to raise their children on their own. A popular explanation for the poverty of single parents in Canada is that most single parents are teenage never-married mothers still in high school, or recently dropped out because of childbirth, and consequently not ready for the job market even if they could get child care.

EATING THE WEDDING GIFTS

It is an appealing explanation because we can once more deplore the irresponsibility (and the morals) of modern adolescents, but it is nonetheless inaccurate. Fewer than 3 percent of female single parents are teenagers, a proportion showing little change over 20 years even as the changing age structure for Canadian society as a whole shows a growing proportion of teenagers, the children of baby boomers.94

This misconception likely owes its considerable staying power to the steady growth of single parents in Canada over 20 years and, even more relevant, to the increase in never-married single parents as part of that growth. While female single parents in total grew from 14 percent of all families with children in 1981 to 20 percent in 2001, the *never-married* portion grew more rapidly from slightly more than one in ten to one in four over the same period.[95] But teenage mothers were not the contributing factor. In fact, as a portion of never-married mothers they declined dramatically.

The proportion of never-married mothers who were between 35 and 45 years of age showed the most significant increase, reflecting in part the early segment of the baby boom cohort moving through this 20-year period. The second largest increase was in the proportion between 25 and 35 years, where the majority of never-married mothers are found. Surprisingly the increase in the 25- to 35-year age group among never-married mothers occurred while that age group was declining in the general population age structure in Canada.

The overrepresentation of the 25- to 35-year age group among never-married single parents may reflect the increasing portion of common-law families among all Canadian families. Over 20 years the number of common-law couples has risen significantly and they now represent 14 percent of all couples, up from 6 percent 20 years ago.[96] Common-law couples can experience marriage breakdown as often as, if not oftener than couples who have been legally married. When it occurs and when children are involved, mothers who become single parents will not differ substantially in age and other characteristics from legally married mothers. They will simply appear in statistics as never married.

Despite public perceptions, teenage mothers cannot be blamed for the growing number of single parents in Canada. This is not to make light of their needs; they face problems of motherhood and adolescence at the same time. Isolation, interrupted education, the early assumption of mature responsibilities, and often the breaking-off of relationships with immediate family are some of the issues they deal with alone. While there is a growing recognition of the need for support services for teenage mothers, they are still left with major decisions to make about the security and development of a young child.

Most teenage mothers now keep their infants rather than placing them for adoption.[97] Once the decision is made, their child care responsibilities keep them at home where they are often supported by social assistance. Making ends meet is added to the list of other issues they face. Among single parents of all ages in Canada, teenage mothers are in the deepest poverty.

Ideally, the identification of causes leads to solutions, but in the case of poverty, a problem that many have wrestled with over the years, the right solution still remains to be found. Causes like a dual labour market and other characteristics of the economic structure are difficult to change. If women don't hold the menial jobs in the economy, who will hold them? Most women would reply—understandably—that filling menial jobs they formerly held is not their problem, or we could expect such a reply at least until women hold the majority of corporate CEO positions and are themselves charged with the responsibility of recruiting a clerical work force. A whole range of labour market changes could take place before that distant day, and the problem might well look after itself. More clerical information may be on-line in the future rather than on paper; more food and hotel services may be automated; more retail cashier services performed by customers themselves. The remaining few menial jobs may, in fact, be in great demand by students who care more about the opportunity to finance university than about the dead-end nature of such jobs.

Other proposed causes of poverty have been misleading. Solving the character deficiencies of the poor appears to be barking up the wrong tree when all the poor need is a good job. When welfare departments devote their efforts to helping recipients find jobs and child care they have more success than when they apply harsh cuts to already low welfare rates in an effort to correct an unwillingness to work that in most cases does not exist. But there is something about the idea of an undeserving mass of poor people that makes many Canadians feel more satisfied with their own accomplishments, so here lies another area resistant to change.

The causes of poverty that are inherent in the divorce process relate only to the poverty of single parents. Solutions to sole custody are already being found, but child support problems are still largely unsolved. As provincial enforcement programs become more effective this may improve, but many single parents would agree their personal financial situation has so far not shown any change.

Looking to the single parents of the future—today's young women leaving high school—it is clear that preventive measures are their best hope in the absence of solutions to single-parent poverty. Taking steps to avoid landing in the low end of the labour market are challenging, but not impossible. Higher education is the fundamental protection. There are several ways to achieve that goal and, despite some obvious struggles and sacrifices, most young women who have reached it agree that the time goes all too quickly.

Barbara Murphy

Chapter 8

POST-SECONDARY EDUCATION, HOW TO GET THERE

Not many young people grow to 18 or 19 years of age without discovering that the unexpected can happen. Routines can be shattered, promises can be broken, certainties can become disappointments. Fortunately these setbacks are few, but each one sharpens our planning skills. Preparing for the unexpected is the whole raison d'être of commercial insurance and, if it were not for the known risks, the insurance industry might also be in the business of insuring new brides against marriage break-up and the poverty of single parenthood.

Post-secondary education, especially university, is one form of insurance for women against the unexpected in marriage and, like all other forms of insurance, it requires an initial outlay. A national survey of Canadian high school graduates found that, although over three-quarters of those who stopped their education at the end of high school gave non-financial reasons, almost a quarter gave the considerable financial outlay as their reason for not going on.[98]

The costs are indeed staggering, but they are not insurmountable. The steady upward trend over the past two decades of Canadian young women going on to university is evidence that many are getting there despite financial barriers that are increasing rather than decreasing. Increases in tuition fees described in Chapter 2—doubling over a decade—have been the result of reduced government spending on post-secondary education institutions. And this extra burden on students has been added over a period when family incomes have remained unchanged (in constant dollars).

The long-term returns on university education are clearly the driving force that overcomes the mounting financial barriers. Women high school students, in particular, have grasped the labour market implications of their decisions after high school. Over 85 percent of female students go on to post-secondary education compared to 78 percent of male students.[99]

With this evidence of above-average female participation, how are women getting around the financial barriers? Like their male counterparts, female high school students have used a number of different methods of financing their university education, including using earnings from jobs since high school graduation, using earnings from jobs while attending high school, getting financial help from parents, applying for scholarships and bursaries, and applying for student loans.

It may be useful to expand on these methods. Although thousands of Canadian students find their way through the post-secondary financing maze each year, the complexity of finding funds should not be taken lightly. A federal government information bulletin begins with this sobering piece of advice: "If you're going on to post-secondary education, bring money."[100] Costs of tuition alone can range from roughly $2,300 in Quebec to $6,400 in Nova Scotia.[101] Books can amount to $1,000.

And there are other costs to consider. When students attend university away from home, they must also find money for up to $6,000 a school year for room and board. Not many students have access to unlimited resources, so decisions about studying in a home town university or one away from home are the earliest decisions to be made.

barbara murphy

Other considerations are the cost of transportation, clothing, and entertainment. Estimating the total, however, is the easy part. Finding the money to cover it comes next.

— • —

Most students make a contribution to the cost of their post-secondary education from their own earnings. Nine out of ten students have employment earnings from summer jobs, according to a recent national survey of student income and expenditures.102 While these earnings were related to summer jobs since finishing high school, another study found that 52 percent of students also used personal savings from wages earned even before they left high school. 103

Canadian students deserve high marks for their contributions from these sources. Student earnings do not come easily. The summer job market is highly competitive for 18- and 19-year-olds finishing high school each June. For one thing, they are already lagging two months behind post-secondary students (mainly 20- to 24-year-olds) who have been out looking for and landing jobs since the end of April. They also lack the work experience of older students. These disadvantages played a larger part in the difficulties faced by new high school graduates in the recession years of the 1990s, keeping their summer employment rates considerably lower than those of post-secondary students. Economic recovery by the end of the century, however, created a healthier labour market for students in the summer. Though older students still catch the better jobs today, the employment rate of new high school graduates has improved.

Consistent with the trend toward greater post-secondary participation by young women, female high school graduates have increasingly found summer jobs to help finance their education. In the 1980s teen-age boys had higher summer employment rates than girls (68 percent compared to 63 percent). By the end of the century the five-point gap had closed; girls were just as likely to find a summer job as boys were.[104]

EATING THE WEDDING GIFTS

Students with a career path in mind have learned that the "transition" summer between high school graduation and first-year university or college is not likely to yield jobs in their chosen field. For the most part, summer jobs for younger students are low-skilled, low-wage jobs. Most employers who count on hiring summer students are in the tourism and food service industries where business expands rapidly over the summer months. Rates of pay are generally minimum wage, although some students have managed to get higher rates.

Students also find summer-specific jobs in camps where counsellors may earn up to $2,000 over two months in out-of-town camps (plus their room and board) and up to $1,200 in city day camps, the rates depending on their location in Canada.

Many business offices also take on extra help over the summer while regular staff take summer vacation. For students lucky enough to get clerical work the rates can often be a little higher than minimum wage.

Employers in these four main areas of summer work are not necessarily looking for work experience or highly developed skills.[105] They list such intangible requirements as the right attitude, a willingness to learn, and the ability to get along with others. In place of work experience, they look in resumés for hobbies and community activities and they are happy to get references from teacher or coaches. In place of skills, they will train. In the food and hospitality business, employers will also trade off both experience and skills for a willingness to work irregular hours. In short, students are just what they are looking for. From the students' perspective, summer jobs may not be challenging or career-oriented but their earnings provide badly needed cash.

Full-time summer work is not the only source of earnings. High school graduates planning to go on to university, especially those who will attend university out of town, must consider part-time employment during the school year as well. Most universities in Canada offer on-campus jobs to

barbara murphy

students. And many students find part-time work in the local community. Almost two-thirds of students work during the school year, for an average of 18 hours a week.[106]

There are mixed reviews on the increasing tendency of students to hold part-time jobs during the school year. Some labour force analysts maintain that employment during high school years is a good thing:

> Entry into the labour force in these years—usually through part-time and/or summer jobs—represents a key transition from childhood to adulthood. Employment for less than 15-20 hours per week does not impede school performance, and indeed a modest level of paid work is associated with better school performance and a lower drop-out rate. Working is positively associated with broader social participation.[107]

But are the same advantages true at the university level? The national survey on student income, referred to earlier, found that employment during the school year had little impact on the academic performance of students and that the number of hours worked also made little difference.[108] Employment, however, did have an effect on the time it took students to complete their studies. Over 40 percent of full-time students indicated they could complete their studies more quickly if they did not have to work.

Some university professors claim that student employment hours during the school year have reached too high a level.[109] Students have little time left to take on supplementary readings, discussions with academic staff, and essays that reflect a thorough exploration of topics. The quality of higher education, they argue, suffers when tight work schedules become the key determinants of the ability of students to study course work beyond the minimum requirements.

If students are stretched to the limit, however, they are not responsible for university financing policies that have placed them in that position. They are responding realistically to a situation that requires a greater student financial contribution than was required in the years of higher learning for the sake of higher learning a generation or two ago. If they see post-secondary education instead as a means to an end in the labour market, it is because Canadian society has also come to see it that way. As one professor noted with some regret: "... there's a more instrumental attitude toward a university education."[110]

Despite these misgivings by academic staff, students are attending universities in increasing numbers each year and many are getting there partly on the strength of their own summer and school-year earnings.

— · —

The second most frequently used source of funds by post-secondary students is the financial assistance of parents.[111] Roughly 88 percent of 18- and 19-year-olds heading from high school to university or college receive support from their parents. While the average amount of parental support is close to $200 a month, many students live at home during the school year receiving a family contribution of room and board that does not show up in most calculations of financial assistance.

Parents are more likely to support younger students and, perhaps related to that, they are more likely to support those without significant employment income. As students get older and bring in better earnings, family support decreases. By the time they reach 22 and 23 years of age the proportion receiving contributions from parents has dropped to three-quarters.[112]

Female students increasingly receive financial assistance from parents although they are still slightly less likely to receive it than male students. This finding could reflect a trace of traditional gender bias still remaining when parents give financial support. Because of labour market wage inequities, the summer employment earnings of female students are also lower than those of men. These disadvantages combined

barbara murphy

appear to have little effect on the predominance of women in post-secondary education. Later in this chapter a discussion of trends in the use of student loans shows that women turn to other available sources of financing.

Despite this stubborn gender difference, the vast majority of women students report parent financial support. Researchers of post-secondary financing acknowledge a large gap in information that would tell us how parents manage to make this contribution. Family incomes have declined in real terms over the past decade while post-secondary costs have shot up dramatically. Savings, therefore, are down, leaving parents strapped for the resources they need to offset the mounting university and college costs in spite of tax deferral incentives for registered education savings plans. Since 1998 parents putting aside savings in such plans have received matched funding from the federal government for a portion of the savings. But this extra contribution from public funds, targeted at a next generation of students, has not been useful for parents of high school graduates today.

In the absence of savings many parents borrow to help finance post-secondary education. They take out bank loans, borrow against lines of credit, or take out second mortgages on their homes. Many parents continue to work following normal retirement age. While these measures clearly will cause hardship for some families, especially those with more than one child enrolled, the more remarkable finding is that so many are making that sacrifice. It illustrates a concern and responsibility for their grown children on the part of Canadian parents that has largely gone unrecognized.[113] Indeed, attitudes about who is responsible for advanced education have changed in recent years. From a collective responsibility for a high standard of education across the country—acknowledging the benefits to society as a whole— we are moving to individual responsibility, acknowledging that many of the benefits of higher education are to private individuals (more on this issue in Chapter 10).

EATING THE WEDDING GIFTS

Other variations in parent contributions have been found. Their contributions are higher for university students than for college students, reflecting higher costs. They are also higher for students who have not received scholarships, bursaries, or loans.

— . —

Scholarships and bursaries are other important sources of student income. Almost a third of high school graduates receive money from scholarships for further education, money that is non-repayable and awarded on the basis of merit in areas that range from outstanding academic achievement to athletics. Usually scholarships are not based on financial need. A further 13 percent of graduates receive bursaries, similar to scholarships in being non-repayable but more often based on financial need.

Graduating students are either put in touch with scholarships through high school guidance counsellors or through Internet searches. There are literally hundreds of scholarships offered, many given by provincial governments (one study gives the average amount of a government grant as $370 a month) and many given by private foundations, universities and colleges, religious organizations, charities, professional associations, business corporations, banks, unions, and well-known organizations like the Royal Canadian Legion, St. John Ambulance, Women's Institute, and others. Some non-government scholarships are more generous than government ones, and some less.

Bursaries are available from sources that are as varied and numerous as scholarships and the list includes sources in every province. They are clearly an important source of financing for students from low and middle income families. A relative newcomer in granting bursaries is the federal government through its Canada Millennium Scholarship Foundation. Over half a million bursaries have been awarded since 1998 ranging in

barbara murphy

amount from $1,000 to $4,500 a year, with the average approximately $3,000. The Foundation gives preference to students in the greatest financial need.

Unfortunately, students are not eligible for Canada Millennium Scholarships until they are a good way through their first year of post-secondary studies, so they are less help to entry students than some other bursaries. Provincial and federal governments work together on these Millennium scholarships, tying them in with student debt, and in some provinces the amount awarded is paid directly to reduce the student's loan.[114]

Searching for scholarships and bursaries is an early exercise in research for students entering university. Most student advisers maintain that the search should be conducted both locally and far afield and that the more dogged the search, the more successful the results will be. With these incentives, students put hours of research into the availability of scholarships and bursaries on top of hours of full-time and part-time work, showing initiative and energy not called upon from their counterparts in previous generations.

—— • ——

It is clear that Canadian students look for more than one source of post-secondary financing. Among young students (up to 20 years of age), over 90 percent use earnings from past and current jobs, 88 percent receive financial assistance from parents, and over 40 percent receive scholarships or bursaries.[115] Nearly every researcher into post-secondary financing emphasizes the importance for students of exploring these non-repayable sources before looking further. Still, when their available funds are totalled, roughly half of students have to borrow for their remaining financial commitments.

Since tuition fees began to rise in the 1990s a great deal has been written about the increasing levels of student debt. A portion of students have always borrowed for their post-secondary education, and the size of that portion has not changed substantially over the years. What has changed is the amount borrowed that students must carry over into their working years after graduation. Graduates in 2000 owed 76 percent more on leaving university than did 1990 graduates, and double the amount owed 20 years earlier.[116]

Many Canadians share a genuine concern about a generation of young people in debt at so early an age. From the perspective of students, given that they are powerless to change formulas that have assigned their share of education costs, the trade-off to the debt burden is the potential benefits they will receive in higher earnings and more challenging jobs over a lifetime. Considering that there has been no reduction in the proportion of students taking out loans while costs rise and that post-secondary education is a voluntary choice, we can only conclude that they consciously choose this direction as part of a lifetime plan.

The debt burden, however, is not insignificant. College graduates and graduates from a university bachelor's program have average debt loads of about $13,000 and $20,000 respectively upon graduation, indicating that many borrowed the maximum loan allowed of $165 a week or $5,000 to $6,000 each year of their studies.[117]

The vast majority of these loans are government loans, with federal and provincial governments sharing the cost of roughly 350,000 student loans each year, shares of 60 percent and 40 percent respectively. Students are not required to begin loan payments until six months after graduation. Two years after graduation, one in five students has paid the loan off completely. The remaining four in five student borrowers pay off almost a quarter of their debt over the next two years. Government lenders point out that this would be the same portion paid off in a standard 10-year loan payment schedule. The majority (three-quarters) of students interviewed across the country did not report difficulties in paying their debt.[118]

The profile of students with government loans reflects the general student population. Over half are granted to students attending university; another 35 percent to students attending

barbara murphy

college.[119] The largest age group receiving loans are students under 21 who receive 44 percent of all government loans. Women receive almost 60 percent of loans (a steadily increasing proportion over the last five years), consistent with their increasing enrolment in post-secondary education.

Looking at the impact of government lending on students from lower-income families, borrowing shows an inconsistent pattern. Government student loans were introduced in 1964 in order to promote access to post-secondary education for students in financial need, but whether access has been improved is not clear cut. Female college and university students from lower-income families[120] appear to borrow more than higher-income students, indicating that the loan program has put more money into the hands of some students with the greatest need. But among males, those from higher-income families borrow more. An explanation might be that males from higher-income families may be more likely to attend institutions out of town, incurring higher costs and increasing the need for borrowing.

Applications for all government student loans are made to provincial loan programs, and individual provinces use their own formulas for calculating the amount to be paid. As a result, loan eligibility may vary from province to province. In general, the loan is calculated by assessing all education and living costs and assessing possible resources the student can bring. The difference between the two is paid out in a loan up to a limit of $210 a week. Provincial differences in assessed costs arise because tuition levels and, in particular, accommodation costs vary across the country. Assessed resources also vary because provinces may have different expectations of student earning amounts and contributions from parents. (Contributions from parents are included in the formula if students are out of high school less than four years.) As a result of varying assessments, the proportion of students borrowing for university, for example, can range from 36 percent in Manitoba to 60 percent in Newfoundland and Labrador.[121]

Student loans are a major source of funding for Canadian post-secondary students. It is significant that student debt has increased as governments have pulled back on funding universities in Canada. Students have become neither more extravagant in their spending habits nor less industrious in their work habits. They are simply borrowing more to pick up the slack of reduced public spending.

Young women graduating from high school are as much involved in this rescue operation as male graduates. They continue to enroll in increasing numbers, taking on their share of the country's university and college costs, and they will expect their share of labour market rewards when their studies are completed.

— · —

A picture emerges of young high school graduates finding their way through the complexities of financing further education. Many don't tackle the problem at all. On the strength of their high school diplomas they take their place in the labour market and leave post-secondary education to others. Only seven percent of those who don't go on claim they choose not to go on because of low grades. Indeed two-thirds of this group give reasons that have nothing to do with financial need or academic standing.[122] In some cases the failure of students to go on to post-secondary education is simply the lack of clear goals. When this is the case, the encouragement of parents can make a difference, as we have seen.

Young women especially are benefitting more than they did in any past generation from the greater attention of parents to their educational futures. Not only parents but other influential people in their lives can help female students through the critical decision-making required, including decisions about financial resources, as high school years come to an end.

Barbara Murphy

$\mathcal{C}hapter\ 9$

ROLE MODELS, COUNSELLORS, AND MENTORS

In the transition to adulthood young people are not completely on their own. Called upon to make important decisions about their futures, they look to certain adults directly or indirectly for information and guidance. In most cases young women will find help and inspiration from adult women; young men, from adult men. These important adults can be role models, counsellors, or mentors, each with their own special way of helping with timely life decisions.

Role models are the traditional influence. Today's parents, more than any other generation of parents, are made aware by professionals in child and adolescent development that they serve as role models for their children. By age five, children are able to identify and differentiate between the roles of their mothers and fathers. And putting gender differences aside, parents collectively make their mark by demonstrating with behaviours, lifestyles, and value systems the way adulthood could look some day, including coping mechanisms for unexpected setbacks along the way.

As role models, parents have a strong influence at every stage of child development. In the sometimes difficult years when their children are teenagers, parents often miss the clues that they still have influence. Instead they become pre-occupied with how the family dynamic is changing as young people look for less supervision and greater independence. Parents struggle to find their new place in this changing environment and complain that, if someone had warned them of the frustrations of parenthood involving adolescents, they would never have signed on. Yet despite these misgivings, studies consistently show parents are the predominant influence on young people.

If a role model is loosely defined as someone worthy of imitation, children may imitate their parents' behaviour through a "social learning" process or they may adopt their values, and often may do both. For example, a major longitudinal study (1970 to 1997) of American young people of three generations found that, despite a great deal of popular concern that social changes (especially more working mothers and increased marriage breakdown) were bringing about the decline of the family and its influence, there has not been a decline in the influence of parents on the educational and career aspirations of young people across generations. In other words, according to the study, families in a changing world find ways to continue to have an influence.[123]

Findings of the study, which followed more than 2,000 individuals over almost thirty years, were not just a confirmation that the generations were equally ambitious in their pursuit of educational and career goals. Present-day young people, the evidence showed, have even higher aspirations than their parents had. A partial explanation lies in broader social changes over the 20th century that have seen each successive generation experience remarkable upward mobility in education. Over the same period employment opportunities have moved from manufacturing to professional and managerial jobs in a similar upward trend. In addition, family size has decreased, providing the latest generation with a greater proportion of parental resources which, in turn, can make aspirations a reality. Whatever the reasons behind this increase in the aspirations of young people, it is clear the influence of a

barbara murphy

parental role model has not declined even in the face of many social changes.

Digging deeper, researchers into the higher aspirations of today's younger generation have found that the increase is largely due to the higher educational and occupational aspirations of young women. Mothers are providing far different role models than they did 20 or 30 years ago. Over a third of the new generation of young women in the above study have grown up with mothers who are college graduates compared with less than half that proportion in the previous generation; almost two-thirds have grown up with mothers who work full time in the labour force compared with less than half that proportion in the previous generation. Roughly 64 percent of young women aspired to professional and managerial occupations a generation ago (24 percent aspired to clerical occupations); today 81 percent have professional/managerial ambitions (only six percent want to be clerks).[124]

If mothers of adolescents today are providing a different role model to what their mothers provided, we have to conclude that a generation ago daughters chose not to imitate their mothers, at least in relation to educational and occupational goals. Indeed, many turned their backs on the full-time homemaking roles their mothers modelled. They chose instead to enter the traditionally male world of work outside the home. These new lifestyles were inspired by principles of equality for women that formed the basis of the new women's movement.

It seems logical to question the strength of role models when so many rejected their mothers' domestic roles in this way in the 1960s and 1970s. Instead of imitating their mothers, the daughters of those decades chose to imitate a handful of activists who came into prominence in Europe and the U.S. During that period Canada, while lacking prominent academic feminists, produced its own crop of influential women seeking change. Doris Anderson, editor of *Chatelaine*, began to shift that magazine's focus away from homemaking to work outside the home, promoting the challenge of independence for a generation of women readers who were ready for it. By the end of the 1960s the report of the Royal Commission on the Status of Women, headed by Florence Bird, provided a further impetus.

There are two answers to the role model reversal that took place a generation ago. The first is that role modelling is not only a process where social learning and imitation take place but is also a process of value transmission. Grandmothers of today's adolescents passed on the value of higher education to their daughters as a route to greater financial independence, equality, and control over their lives than they had enjoyed themselves. Those grandmothers belonged, in fact, to the same generation as the new wave of academic feminists (Friedan, de Beauvoir, Greer, etc.) and shared their values and frustrations. Assigned to domestic roles themselves, women outside academia could still think, read, and be influenced by new ideas about a more equal role for women in society. If their own situation did not allow them to provide a role model of the financially independent working woman to imitate, many mothers in the 1960s and 1970s influenced their daughters by identifying with the feminist values of equality and independence.

A second answer to the apparent rejection of mother role models in the 1960s and 1970s is that young women can have strong secondary role models outside the family. The new prominent feminists provided such models for that generation. History is full of examples of role models not personally known to young people, from Joan of Arc to Laura Secord to Florence Nightingale. Literature of the past provided Jane Eyre, strong-willed governess at Thornfield, and Scarlett O'Hara, indomitable saviour of Tara; newspaper comic pages provided Jane Arden, ace reporter who felt as comfortable calling her boss *Chief* in the 1930s as did her male colleagues. In young adult literature teenage girls have found a role model in amateur detective Nancy Drew for three generations, all finding something to emulate in this clever and resourceful young woman whose father (a single parent) obligingly leaves her to her own devices for incredibly long periods of time.

barbara murphy

Besides historical and fictitious characters, role models are increasingly found in today's multi-media. Most teenage girls would have no difficulty in identifying popular role models such as Keira Knightly, Julia Styles, Beyoncé, Jennifer Garner, Jessica Alba, and Mandy Moore, whose clothing, hair styles and personalities are much imitated. Career role models made popular through the media are, among others, Roberta Bondar, one of the first women in space, Margaret Atwood, novelist, and Belinda Stronach, business executive and politician. While these are real-life career role models, future forensic scientists might be inspired by mother and scientist Catherine Willows in the television series, *Crime Scene Investigation*.

From parents to celebrities, a wide range of role models are available. By inspiring and modelling, and sometimes advising and supporting, they help young women to see what is possible and to make decisions about what to keep and what to discard in the opportunities facing them.

While role models may inspire, school personnel give help in other ways. The most relevant staff are guidance counsellors, trained practitioners whose job descriptions include not only direct counselling of students but serving as a resource for parents and teachers. Like parents, they have the advantage over celebrities of knowing personally the students they guide. Most guidance counsellors who are not spread too thin are a valuable resource for up-to-date information on where students can find the most relevant programs for their post-secondary plans.

The National Occupational Classification job description for a guidance ("educational") counsellor lists the following duties:[125] counselling students about educational issues such as course and program selection while in high school, counselling students about career or vocational issues including career planning, and making available to students a wide range of educational and occupational information. This information can also be made available to parents but this part of information-sharing is not always a priority (see below). Part of the guidance counsellor's work is to help students identify interests and abilities and, for that purpose, they may use special aptitude tests. Nearly all counsellors are involved in the orientation programs given by universities or colleges for high school students, and they keep themselves up to date on academic programs they offer.

But their capacity to reach out to individual students uncertain about their future plans should not be overestimated. A study prepared for the federal government found the lack of one-on-one counselling by school guidance counsellors to be a serious drawback in four provinces sampled.[126] Students interviewed expressed the need for more individualized help with connecting post-secondary entrance requirements and courses of study with a career direction. Maintaining that a lack of career direction was a more serious problem for their children than financial resources, parents interviewed for the study also had expectations of more one-on-one help from counsellors. They not only looked for this help in career planning from school guidance staff, they wanted to be involved and felt such opportunities were lacking.

Despite their dissatisfaction with the role of guidance counsellors in individual career decision-making, both students and parents found them a good source of general information about post-secondary opportunities, very likely a clue to the emphasis placed by local school boards on one of these functions over the other. Not surprisingly, the study concluded that the capacity of guidance counsellors to fulfull all their functions should be increased by adding more staff to guidance programs.

And still within the high school setting, teachers can also be counsellors for students in making their career plans. Teachers have the closest personal knowledge of the abilities of individual students and are often the ones to make students aware of their potential. Many adults can look back on their school years and recall a particular teacher who made the connection for them between their strongest academic subjects and a future career. Secondary school teachers, in particular, claim that such not-too-rare examples of advice and guidance acted upon by students are among the most satisfying parts of their jobs.

While the three major (and officially recognized) components of a secondary school teacher's job are to prepare, instruct, and evaluate, most teachers would agree that learning often fails to take place without motivation. So implicit is the skill of motivating students in a learning situation, it is often mentioned as a required skill but rarely mentioned as a function of the teacher's role.[127] Using their motivational skills in career guidance, teachers can have a powerful influence on a young person uncertain about their future goals.

Unfortunately, as illustrated in studies in Chapter 2, teachers sometimes have lower post-secondary expectations for women students than for men, especially young women in lower-income families, simply because they assume financial support is not equally available. With this mindset, they may not be as inclined to motivate female students to further their education even though they may have the academic qualifications. Clearly these are the very students who need the extra personal support.

Whatever the assumptions of teachers, vocational guidance and career planning are not the primary functions of their jobs. They are the functions of guidance counsellors, and the importance placed on this function in high schools across the country will naturally vary according to financial resources and local priorities.

— • —

One of the more exciting developments over the past 15 years has been the increased interest in mentoring as an effective approach to reaching young women making career decisions. Mentoring's recent origins are in business where the development of relatively inexperienced staff is crucial to creating a pool of future leaders in an increasingly competitive market-place. Without the incentive of profits, the public sector has had decreased revenues to contend with and has a similar interest in making the most of their human resources. By the mid-1990s the federal Treasury Board had in place a comprehensive set of guidelines for the development of mentoring programs in government departments. Public education and higher education were also in the process of exploring the uses of mentoring in improving student-teacher relations, student-faculty relations, and professional development of new staff.

These origins, however, are recent. The word *mentor* comes from Homer's *Odyssey* in which Ulysses entrusts his son to his friend Mentor while he undertakes his famous voyage. Mentor is to guide the son in his passage from boyhood to manhood, helping him with all the personal development and identity tasks of that important transition. Today mentoring is still a process of supporting and influencing personal growth and development while expanding to accommodate the continuing need for professional development.

Women, especially, have found mentoring to be an effective way to overcome the visible and invisible barriers to career progress in a male-dominated work world. In early mentoring relationships, usually informal, senior career women shared with juniors their experience of finding their way through the organization and coping with its unique power relations. But not every junior staff member sought out a mentor, and not every senior staff member was willing to share the lessons she had learned. More formal mentoring relationships—arranged pairings—between women have overcome most of this reticence as an increasing number of successful women are willing to pass on their expertise.

The simplest definition of a mentoring relationship is the pairing of an experienced person with a less experienced one for the purpose of support, development and growth. While business, government, and education have recently put such

barbara murphy

pairings into practice, some social service organizations have been using mentoring for years in Homer's original context of supporting young people in the transition from adolescence to adulthood. The services of Big Brothers Big Sisters (which were originally separate organizations) include the matching of children and adolescents with adults for this purpose. When they began early in the 20th century these programs were aimed at youth who had come into contact with juvenile courts for one reason or another. Churches and businesses in Toronto, as early as 1913, came together to form a voluntary organization to help young offenders, especially those from father-absent homes. Following the lead of the American founders of Big Brothers, associations in Canada were formed in many cities over the next 50 years. Changes in the focus of Big Brothers in Canada were introduced in the 1950s when matching services were extended to all boys lacking a male influence in their lives whether or not they had been referred through the courts.

Over the years Big Sisters organizations have also been introduced in communities in Canada to provide supportive relationships between girls and female adults. Big Brothers and Big Sisters joined their programs in many of those communities by the 1970s. Today more than 300 communities are served across the country with hundreds of committed volunteers providing the role of mentors.

Does it all work? Recent evaluations of Big Brothers Big Sisters programs have come up with the following findings: the children and young people served in mentoring programs graduate from high school at a rate of 20 percent higher than the national average; 78 percent of those who were on social assistance (or their families were on assistance) no longer rely on this form of income; and a disproportionately high number of young people served in the programs graduated from college or university compared with others in their age group.[128]

Big Brothers and Big Sisters are the original mentors of children and adolescents although their target group has generally been helping those at risk, and the goal has been to deal with self-esteem issues. A special mentoring program in Ottawa, in partnership with the Youth Services Bureau, has an added focus of strengthening the child or adolescent's school learning skills and increasing school attendance. Mentors in the *Mentoring InSchool Partnership Program* are paired individually with students and meet with them weekly on school premises.

More recently Big Brothers Big Sisters have introduced special mentoring programs to help this same target group make the transition from school to work. Programs for this purpose, called Mobilizing Community Partners, operate in Burlington and Edmonton, and there may be other communities not yet posted. Youth are matched with mentors in the work force and given workplace exposure. Employers play an important role, allowing mentors in their organizations to give time and attention to the task of letting high school students learn first hand some of the skills and further education required for their chosen occupation. Although programs vary, students can spend three to four hours every week with a mentor in the workplace. Results have shown that the programs have helped students in their decision-making with regard to their future careers.

A mentoring program offered by the YWCA in Vancouver is directly aimed at career planning for young women. With the purpose of helping grade 11 and 12 students make the transition from high school to career, the Y program matches young women with professional women who will meet with them regularly through the school year to share information about their own careers. In the process high school students also have opportunities to job-shadow their mentors during the work day. The YWCA Mentoring Program, in operation since 1991, has found mentors for over 1,000 young women, generally 15 to 18 years of age. With guidance, advice, and support from mentors, these young women explore career options and learn the educational requirements they must meet to reach their goals.

barbara murphy

In Toronto the busy Women in Motion Career Education organization offers several programs to help with career planning. Specifically aimed at female high school students, the Step Up and Lead mentoring program pairs students with professional women in a variety of occupations for the purpose of career advice, goal setting, and firsthand observation of the job in action.[129]

Professional women in this program volunteer their time, sharing their own experiences through weekly meetings with students. In addition, students job-shadow their mentors including attendance at conferences and meetings. Out of the three-month mentoring relationship offering considerable exposure to the workplace comes a number of other advantages. Women students begin to see the relevance of academic subjects to the world of work when the relationship has often been obscure in the classroom. They see the gaps that must still be filled with higher education. They also begin to envision themselves in the job of their dreams. To that end they are connected through their mentor with other professional women and can begin to build a network of contacts that can be drawn upon when they finally prepare to enter the work force.

Step Up and Lead is a non-profit organization as are most mentoring programs. With its major sponsor the Institute of Chartered Accountants of Ontario, its female volunteers tend to be professionals in business, finance, and technology, and its recruits are students wishing to explore these fields. Female students who go on to information technology training specifically are also helped by the organization's Link-I-T program which provides one-to-mentorship relationships with women workers in the high tech field.

The well-known Operation Minerva program in Alberta now has over 15 years' experience in providing mentors for young women. In the late 1980s when it came into existence it was intended to address a concern of science teachers and women scientists that young women were not taking high school science and mathematics courses in great numbers and, as a result, very few women were going on to university programs in science and technology in preparation for careers in those fields.

Responding to these concerns, the Operation Minerva program was founded for the purpose of providing mentors for Grade 8 girls who would soon be making course decisions on entering high school. Mentors are women working in science and technology careers in a wide range of specializations including geophysics, engineering, dentistry, veterinarian medicine, forensics, medicine, and geology. Each mentor spends a job-shadowing day with two Grade 8 students, introducing them to related work in the office, field or laboratory. Program coordinators claim that the whole experience is more valuable if students actually observe problem-solving that would make up part of the scientist's regular work day.[130]

Program results have been extremely positive. More female students in Alberta are entering engineering and medical programs and some part of these increases may be due to the fact that the program has reached hundreds of young women over 15 years. More directly, however, the program has undergone a formal evaluation of its success in meeting the original goals with quite clear results. Over 90 percent of Operation Minerva participants have pursued three or more science courses at the secondary school level. Roughly 73 percent are pursuing at least one science course at university. And 82 percent of past Operation Minerva participants state they would consider a future science career.[131]

As influences on young women, mentors in all the above career planning programs are both role models and counsellors, doubly effective because their inspiration and advice takes place in a workplace setting. The programs using this approach, offered in a few communities across Canada, begin to fill a gap for young women looking to the future in their high school years. Women mentors who take part are rewarded with the satisfaction of making even a small difference in a young woman's life and many report this is what keeps them in the program year after year.

barbara murphy

On the other hand, not every working woman can make that ongoing commitment. Mentoring programs are so heavily reliant on volunteers that turnover and recruiting problems are a constant challenge to existing programs and a serious consideration for organizations wanting to start new ones. Turnover is not so much a function of the nature of the mentoring experience (indeed, evaluations show satisfaction is extremely high) as of the time pressures on busy working adults, many of whom are parents of adolescents themselves. Most mentors would also include the investment of energy and emotions as a factor that can sometimes keep them from participating as often as they would like. There are also program coordination costs sometimes covered by private or public sector funders, and these costs are not always secure. As a result, recruiting and funding difficulties limit the growth of these programs and not every young woman in every community has the opportunity to benefit.

——— • ———

The help of role models, counsellors, and mentors is meant to make career planning a shared project for young women. Some helping adults have formal training that includes learning what teenagers consider important (and often teenagers do not rank career planning high in importance). For other helping adults, learning about the primary concerns of teenagers is less formal. They may read extensively on the subject or they may reach back into memories of their own adolescence to understand what is going on in the minds of today's younger generation. Whether their preparation is formal or informal, most role models, counsellors, and mentors find they cannot be effective if they ignore other adolescent priorities that compete with career planning.

High on the list of priorities is the process of self-identity. Any helping relationship is affected by this important part of teenage development. It is a work-in-progress for most adolescents, and it usually involves a considerable amount of trial

EATING THE WEDDING GIFTS

and error, trying to find a *persona* that feels right, filtering reactions, and moving haltingly toward a full knowledge of themselves. It goes without saying these trials are played out among their peers and to a lesser extent among the adults in their sphere of relationships at home, school, part-time work and leisure activities. In the midst of this life-stage task, role models, counsellors, and mentors introduce their concern about the future beyond high school at their own peril. It is as distracting as asking someone running an obstacle course how they feel about their next race when they are not entirely convinced they will finish the current one.

But distracting though it may be, in the midst of this identity formation young women have to focus at least some of their attention on the future. Even throughout high school they have been bringing a preference for impulsive behaviour more and more under control, making course selections that might affect future choices, allocating the necessary time to assignments that will bring a satisfactory grade. In their minds all this self-control is sometimes being brought to bear to reach goals that are someone else's, not their own. When they are urged to look to the future, to think about higher education and career, it is perhaps understandable that they still believe such forward-thinking is someone else's idea of an important goal.

The control young women are learning in adolescence is just in time. They are expected at this stage of their lives to move into self-regulated adult behaviour that calls on inner controls of their own making and less reliance on external rules. This is one forward step that meets with their hearty approval. Independence becomes a pressing priority. Indeed, adolescents think they are more ready for self-made rules than the rest of the world thinks they are. Unfortunately, while they assume these new responsibilities, advice and guidance are often mistaken for standards imposed by others, a regressive development to be resisted on the path to independence. We ask them to think for themselves, but we fail to make it clear that, even as adults, we turn to others for advice without making us any less adult.

Barbara Murphy

The priorities of young women also include romantic relationships, which have a stronger influence on planning for the future than we sometimes take into account. In Chapter 2 the attraction of marriage for young women was suggested as a factor in some choosing not to go on to university at the end of high school. The Operation Minerva mentoring program, described earlier, found that some of the questions of grade 8 (!) students about occupations in science and engineering revealed their concern about integrating a science career with family life. There is no easy answer to this competing priority, except to point out to young romantics that all university students are not celibate and that one can be in love and study at the same time. In fact, many women meet their future husbands while at university.

Clearly there are difficulties inspiring, guiding, and advising young women, but the rewards are great, especially for the young women themselves. Navigating a course through their other higher-ranking priorities is not impossible for helping adults. Half the battle is acknowledging the legitimacy of what is important to them and identifying with these life-stage challenges by recalling our own adolescent years.

EATING THE WEDDING GIFTS

Chapter 10

CHOICES AND RESPONSIBILITIES

In most cases advice and support are available to young women about to leave high school. Indeed, the attention of others is a good indication of the importance attached to this stage of a young person's life. But although advice and support are available, it is also a time for decision-making that is essentially personal. No two women look at the range of choices from the same social background. No two women bring the same personality attributes into the equation.

One of the key variables of social background is the value placed on education by everyone with influence during growing years. Like all values, the value of education passes quietly into a child's repertoire of things that seem right and proper almost without notice. So intangible are these legacies that many adults cannot recall when they began to claim them as part of their own value system.

The personality trait that most often comes to the rescue of adolescents in the transition to adulthood is the capacity to delay short-term goals in favour of those that will only be realized in the future. Young women are expected to pull this show of personal strength out of a hat when, in fact, their 18 to 20 years of experience have not regularly required such a trade-off. Compulsory schooling, rules (often without reasons), and only a guarded respect for original ideas from the young do not always provide a breeding ground for the development of self-discipline and long-range planning. But many women make the shift at this transition stage and learn to reconcile conflicting demands.

If, in the end, decisions are personal, the role of information becomes even more crucial. Young women need to be aware that the timetable for marriage and motherhood can be safely put off for a number of years, that the man of their dreams will still be there, that their biological clocks are not in danger of running out, that they will enjoy motherhood more with a little maturity, and that a whole generation of women are marrying later based on these assurances.

What cannot be assured is that any marriage, early or late, will last. Early ones, however, are more likely to fail, a pattern that has held for over 30 years of overall divorce rate fluctuations.[132] The contributing factors to the break-up of early marriages appear to be less than mature judgment about the choice of partners, the arrival of children at an age when the accompanying responsibilities and sacrifices run counter to a desire for freer lifestyles, and a tendency for younger couples to have lower family incomes and greater financial pressures that one or both partners may want to leave behind.

Information about these realities is important to the decision-making process. Not many of us, however, want to rain on parades when young women weigh the benefits of early marriage (moving away from home, sharing life with someone who cares, even the lure of a dream wedding and the prospect of being "queen for a day") against the less exciting benefits of three or four years of study that society has imposed on anyone wanting to earn a good salary. But if decision-making is not informed, if we mistakenly believe they are better off without the sobering facts, young female high school graduates may head into early marriages with

EATING THE WEDDING GIFTS

a 50 percent chance of success and, if they should fall victim to those odds, they will become single parents with a 90 percent chance of raising their children in poverty.

Poverty has become predominantly a female issue in Canada and other advanced countries. But men who take leadership roles in society's economic, political, and social institutions have little incentive to turn things around. Women, on the other hand, would have everything to gain if the feminization of poverty were to be solved, but they are seldom in positions of power. Although they have become increasingly aware of wage inequities that hold them to poverty-level incomes, they are powerless to change the situation single-handedly or overnight. The most pragmatic approach is to educate themselves out of the low-wage jobs reserved for them in the labour force.

Better salaries leave women in a more enviable position if their marriage breaks up. Not only can they put food on the table, they can put better food on the table. While child care costs force low-wage women out of their jobs and onto welfare, those with higher salaries pay their own sitters and continue to work.

If women graduating from high school cannot imagine themselves in poverty, other benefits of higher education may offer a greater incentive. Undergraduate courses at university develop skills that can be transferred and used in every part of life, not just the economic sphere. A higher level of critical thinking grows out of the challenge of academic courses that allow the freedom to question old truths. Graduates report more confidence in analyzing conventional wisdoms in the world outside the walls of university and reshaping their own opinions. At the same time, with their new confidence they tend to have a greater appreciation for the diversity of society based on a broader understanding of its sources. Opinions, then, tend to be their own but open to challenge and change.

Also outside the economic world university graduates tend to read more, write better, and vote with greater frequency. They enjoy a certain amount of personal status by virtue of

barbara murphy

all these skills gained through higher education, and their children tend to do well at school. Their transferable skills also allow university graduates more freedom than other workers have to move around, change jobs, even to relocate.

Knowledge of these and other facts are what women need for their important decisions following high school. They are increasingly making these decisions in favour of the more secure personal future offered by higher education than the future they can expect without it. In doing so, they continue a trend that began with the individual actions of women, not with far-sighted policies of governments or higher education institutions. If anything, the most dramatic gains for women in post-secondary education have taken place during a period when earlier accessibility policies (for all students, not just women) have all but been abandoned.

In making these decisions, growing numbers are rejecting women's traditional developmental pattern of preparing for marriage and motherhood to the exclusion of their own need for a productive and challenging personal life and a broader role in society than the domestic role of earlier generations. One researcher who followed the decisions made by a group of women in their 20s in the early period of this trend writes:

> Those who have eschewed the domestic model have unwittingly set in motion a self-reinforcing process that changes the situation for all women. As women have increasingly vacated the home for the workplace those left behind have found themselves having to defend an increasingly devalued way of life.[133]

Although the situation has been changed for all women, the fact that each female student today makes her own choice should not be underestimated. There is still room for providing information, for laying out the pluses and minuses that will make her decision easier.

— • —

EATING THE WEDDING GIFTS

Will women continue to take one of two directions after high school? The answer depends partly on the social attitudes of the more fortunate women who take the path to higher education and better economic futures. In Chapter 1 the review of two demographic trends involving women—one a positive trend, the other negative—showed that these developments have occurred quite independently, as if the lucky and the unlucky were not aware of the others' existence. Although all these women lived in the same country, in the same cities, and at one time went to the same high schools, they live in different worlds now. This social distance leaves a great deal of room for indifference on the part of successful women about the plight of single parents living in poverty and it risks the inevitable outcome of out of sight, out of mind.

It is one thing to demonstrate that women can take separate paths when they leave high school. It is quite another to accept the two different worlds they finally come to occupy as fair and just outcomes of the choices they made. Too many life events intervene to hold each high school graduate totally accountable for her decision.

Women who have chosen higher education and gone on to a successful career have moved into leadership roles in society whether they intended to or not. And their new roles carry with them social responsibilities, among them the need to keep poverty on the public agenda. With the growing feminization of poverty caused by inequities in the labour market and unequal sharing of the child care burden, non-poor women need to look out for poor women regardless of the choices made when they were young adults.

University degrees come with responsibilities attached if for no other reason than society's contribution to the costs of higher education. While we watch with concern the diminishing size of that contribution, it is considerable nonetheless. In Canada, student contributions of almost a fifth of the cost of post-secondary education are still far short of the actual cost. Another fifth is covered by donations and endowments of generous Canadians. The remaining 60 per-

barbara murphy

cent is paid by Canadian taxpayers, among them workers in low-income jobs who would be hard pressed to come up with a list of benefits to themselves and their families of a highly educated group of workers who reap a disproportionate share of society's resources. Taxpayers may pitch in collectively to pay for higher education, but the financial rewards that come out at the other end are not always spread evenly across society.

It is true there are public benefits. The higher salaries of university-educated workers increase national tax revenues and maintain high consumption levels that make for job creation and a healthier economy. But private benefits to the university-educated wage earner are substantially greater. University graduates not only make a larger contribution to national consumption, their increased purchases of consumer goods translate into a higher standard of living than that of workers with high school education. They have higher employment rates throughout their working lives, improved working conditions in the form of white-collar work and consistent hours, better general health, and longer life expectancy. These are essentially private gains made as a result of considerable public outlay. Enjoying them, university graduates have to guard against short memories.

It can be argued that indifference, even apathy, continues to delay any solution to the problem of single-parent poverty in Canada. Women make up more than half the voting-age population and 20 percent of them now have university degrees. Yet cuts to welfare payments—almost 40 percent are to women and their children—have been introduced in most provinces without a murmur from the female-dominated electorate, and child care spaces for low-income mothers have been reduced over a decade with such ease that one suspects governments believe such measures can be taken without fear of voter disapproval. Federal shares in this spending have also been reduced and successive federal governments appear to feel little pressure despite the fact there are over three-quarters of a million more females of voting age than males.[134]

EATING THE WEDDING GIFTS

There is a certain amount of irony in this apparent indifference of women who are gaining economically and enjoying the benefits of fair hiring and equal pay laws that have only come about in response to a strong women's movement of over 30 years. The same women's movement has also boasted that greater representations of women in all our social institutions will bring a greater sense of humanity than men have been able to bring to society's many problems. Where are these humane women hiding?

Rather than hiding they appear to be preoccupied with their own battles. Women's victories on the economic front may still not be large enough or permanent enough to let them turn this sense of humanity loose in solving the problems of other women. Fear of losing gains can consume an inordinate amount of energy. Remaining optimistic, we can only hope a new generation of successful women may be able to relax their vigilance and redirect some of this energy to the problems of those who have not been as fortunate.

barbara murphy

Endnotes

CHAPTER 1

1. National Council of Welfare, *Poverty Profile,* August 1999, p. 38.

2. National Council of Welfare, *Poverty Profile*, 1999.

3. Statistics Canada, *Lone-parent Families in Canada*, 1992.

4. *Lone-parent Families in Canada.*

5. Statistics Canada, *Earnings of Canadians: Making a living in the new economy,* 2001.

6. Marion Porter, John Porter, and B. Glishen, *Does Money Matter? Prospects for Higher Education in Ontario,* 1979.

7. S. Baliga and S. Goyal, "Education and marriage age: Theory and evidence," *EconPapers*, University of Munich, 2002.

8. Vanier Institute of the Family, *Profiling Canada's Families II,* 2000.

9. R. Phillips, *Putting Asunder: A history of divorce in Western society,* 1988.

10. *Putting Asunder*, p. 402.

11. *Putting Asunder*, p. 616.

12. Vanier Institute of the Family, *Profiling Canada's Families II,* 2000.

13. James G. Snell, *In the Shadow of the Law: Divorce in Canada, 1900-1939,* 1991.

14. Statistics Canada, Canada Year Book, *Break-up*, 2003.

15. Statistics also fail to record the break-up of common-law unions, a family formation which increased by 26 percent in the last decade of the 20th century, according to the Vanier Institute of the Family, while the rate of legal marriages declined. With the many children born in common-law unions, thousands of female partners join the ranks of single parents at time of break-up.

16. Grace Lockhart, the first woman to receive a university degree in Canada.

17. Margaret Gillett, *We Walked Very Warily: A History of Women at McGill*, 1981.

18. Gillett, p. 7.

19. Gillett, p. 15.

20. Gillett, p. 15.

21. Gillett, p. 287.

22. Lesley A. Bellamy and Neil Guppy, "Opportunities and obstacles for women in Canadian higher education," in *Women and Education,* J.S. Gaskell and A.T. McLaren, eds., 1991.

23. "Mrs. Langstaff cannot practice law, is decision," *Montreal Herald*, 13 February 1915, quoted in Gillett.

24. Gillett, p. 322.

25. Porter, Porter, and Blishen, *Does Money Matter?* 1979; Bellamy and Guppy, "Opportunities and obstacles for women in Canadian higher education," 1991.

26. Paul Anisef et al., *Opportunity and Uncertainty, Life Course Experiences of the Class of '73*, 2000.

CHAPTER 2

27. Paul Anisef et al., *Opportunity and Uncertainty,* 2000; E. Dianne Looker, "Active capital: The impact of parents on youths' educational performance and plans," in *Sociology of Education in Canada*, Lorna Erwin and David MacLennan, eds., 1994; Paul Anisef and Norman Okihoro, *Losers and Winners*, 1982.

28. *Losers and Winners*, 1982, p. 82.

29. *Opportunity and Uncertainty*, 2000.

30. While these were outcomes for those who completed high school, some educators argue that many immigrants with poor English language skills are dropping out before completion. See Andrew Duffy, "Why are ESL students being left behind?" *Ottawa Citizen*, October 23, 2004, p. E16.

EATING THE WEDDING GIFTS

31. Trevor H. Williams, "Educational aspirations: Longitudinal evidence on their development in Canadian youth," *Sociology of Education*, 45, 1972.

32. Porter, Porter, and Blishen, *Does Money Matter?* 1979.

33. Looker, Active Capital: "The impact of parents on youths' educational performance and plans."

34. *Opportunity and Uncertainty*, 2000.

35. Looker, "The impact of parents on youths' educational performance."

36. Looker, "The impact of parents on youths' educational performance."

37. Porter, Porter, and Blishen, *Does Money Matter?*

38. Statistics Canada, *University Financial Statistics.*

39. Canada, Standing Committee on Human Resources Development and the Status of Persons with Disabilities, *Interim Report, Access to Higher Education and Training,* 2000.

40. *Interim Report, Access to Higher Education and Training.*

CHAPTER 3

41. Statistics Canada, *Lone-parent Families in Canada*, 1992.

42. Statistics Canada, *Earnings of Canadians, Making a Living in the New Economy,* 2001.

43. Pat Armstrong, Hugh Armstrong, *The Double Ghetto, Canadian Women and Their Segregated Work*, 1994. In this study service industries are defined as trade; finance, insurance and real estate; community, business, and personal services; and public administration and defense.

44. Statistics Canada, W*omen and the Canadian Labour Market,* 1998; Armstrong and Armstrong, *The Double Ghetto*, 1994.

45. *Women and the Canadian Labour Market,* 1998.

46. *The Globe and Mail*, March 27, 2004.

47. Ceta Ramkhalawansingh, "Women during the Great War," in *Women at Work 1850-1930*, 1974.

barbara murphy

48. Elizabeth Graham, "Schoolmarms and early teaching in Ontario," in *Women at Work 1850-1930*.

49. Seventy such schools existed in Canada by 1900, according to Judi Coburn's history of nursing in *Women at Work 1850-1930*.

50. Graham S. Lowe, "Women, work and the office: the feminization of clerical occupations in Canada, 1901-1931," *Canadian Journal of Sociology*, 1980; Statistics Canada, *Women and the Canadian Labour Market*, 1998.

51. Canada, *Services 2000*.

52. Economic Council of Canada, *Good Jobs, Bad Jobs, Employment in the Service Economy*, 1990.

53. In fact, women entering occupations requiring university education made the greatest contribution to the growth in the Canadian labour force over the past ten years, according to Statistics Canada.

54. *Women and the Canadian Labour Market*.

55. *Women and the Canadian Labour Market*.

56. Human Resources Development Canada, *National Occupational Classification*.

CHAPTER 4

57. Childcare Resource and Research Unit, *Early Childhood Education and Care in Canada 2001*, 2002.

58. *Early Childhood Education and Care in Canada 2001*.

59. *Early Childhood Education and Care in Canada 2001*.

60. Statistics Canada, *Work Activity of Parents, Age Groups of Children, and Family Structure for Children of Lone-parent Families*, 2001; *Early Childhood Education and Care in Canada 2001*.

61. In these provincial breakdowns, figures on subsidized spaces are taken from *Early Childhood Education and Care in Canada 2001*; figures on children under 12 of working single parents are provided by Statistics Canada.

62. Gordon Cleveland and Michael Krashinsky, *Our Children's Future, Child Care Policy in Canada*, 2001.

EATING THE WEDDING GIFTS

63. Canada, *National Child Benefits Report*, 2002; Statistics Canada, 2001 Census.

64. National Council of Welfare, *Profiles of Welfare: Myths and Realities*, 1998.

65. For an interesting account of life on minimum wage in the U.S., see Barbara Ehrenreich, *Nickel and Dimed, On (Not) Making out in America*, 2001. The author spent several months undercover as a minimum wage worker in three cities.

66. Canadian Association of Food Banks, *Hunger Count 2003*.

67. Nova Scotia Department of Community Services, Employment Support and Income Assistance, *Schedule A, Personal Allowance and Maximum Shelter Allowance.*

68. Canada Mortgage and Housing, *Canadian Housing Statistics 2002.* Information in this chapter on average rental costs in all cities is taken from *Canadian Housing Statistics 2002.*

69. Saskatchewan, *Social Assistance Handbook.*

70. Community Development Halton, T*he Social Assistance Reform Act: An Information Package,* 1998.

71. Edmonton Social Planning Council, *Welfare and the Cost of Living*, 2004.

72. National Council of Welfare, *Profiles of Welfare: Myths and Realities.*

73. Canadian Council on Social Development, *Canadian Welfare Incomes as a Percentage of the Poverty Line by Family Type and Province, 2001.*

74. "Premier apologizes to welfare recipients," *Ottawa Citizen*, April 17, 1998, p. A6.

75. "Laughing all the way to the food bank," *Ottawa Citizen*, September 21, 1998, p. A11.

CHAPTER 6

76. Steven P. Martin, *Unequal trends in marital stability: Women's educational attainment and marital dissolutions involving young children from 1975 to 1995*, Department of Sociology, University of Maryland, 2000.

barbara murphy

CHAPTER 7

77. George Gilder, *Wealth and Poverty*, 1980; Charles Murray, *Losing Ground, American Social Policy 1950-1980*, 1984; and Lawrence Mead, *Beyond Entitlement, The Social Obligations of Citizenship*, 1986.

78. In Canada poverty researchers were content with arguing that, because measurements were faulty, there really was very little poverty at all. See Christopher Sarlo, *Poverty in Canada* 1994.

79. Economic Council of Canada, *The New Face of Poverty, Income Security Needs of Canadian Families*, 1992.

80. William J. Wilson, *When Work Disappears, the World of the New Urban Poor,* 1996. In this Urban Poverty and Family Life Study, poor neighbourhoods were defined as those neighbourhoods in which a substantial majority of individual adults were either unemployed or had dropped out of the labour force altogether. They also included census tracts in which at least 20 percent of residents had family incomes below the federal poverty line.

81. A. Kazemipur and S.S. Halli, *The New Poverty in Canada, Ethnic Groups and Ghetto Neighbourhoods*, 2000.

82. Statistics Canada, *Women in Canada,* 2000. The remaining 11 percent were other custodial arrangements, grandparents, etc.

83. Statistics Canada, *Daily*, May 4, 2004.

84. Statistics Canada, *Daily*, June 2, 1998.

85. Quoted in David A. Klein, *Family Law Awards in Canada*, 1987.

86. Justice Canada, *Custody, Access and Child Support: Findings from the National Longitudinal Survey of Children and Youth*, 1998.

87. Eleventh Annual Conference of the Children's Rights Council, October 23-26, 1997.

88. Judith A. Seltzer, "Father by law: Effects of joint legal custody on nonresident fathers' involvement with children," *Demography*, 35 (2), 1998.

89. Statistics Canada, *Child and Spousal Support: Maintenance Enforcement Survey*, 2002-3.

90. "Deadbeat parents owe $1.3 billion, Auditor," *Canadian Press*, December, 2003.

EATING THE WEDDING GIFTS

91. "True deadbeat dads are few, Ottawa says," *Toronto Star,* September 6, 1995.

92. Statistics Canada, *Child and Spousal Support: Maintenance Enforcement Survey Statistics*, 2002-3.

93. National Council of Welfare, *Poverty Profile 1997*, Autumn 1999.

94. Statistics Canada, *Women in Canada*, 2000.

95. *Women in Canada.*

96. Statistics Canada, *Daily*, October 22, 2002.

97. Vanier Institute of the Family, *Profiling Canada's Families II,* 2004.

CHAPTER 8

98. E. Dianne Looker, *Why Don't They Go On? Factors Affecting the Decisions of Canadian Youth Not to Pursue Post-secondary Education,* prepared for the Canada Millennium Scholarship Foundation, 2001.

99. Statistics Canada, *Who goes to post-secondary education and when: Pathways chosen by 20-year-olds*, 2003.

100. Industry Canada, Money Savvy 101, Lesson 2, *Consumer Connection*, 2004.

101. Canadian Association of College and University Student Services, *Guide to University Costs in Canada,* 2004. Other provincial average tuition costs are Newfoundland $3,000, PEI $4,800, New Brunswick $5,000, Ontario $4,800, Manitoba $3,300, Saskatchewan $4,900, Alberta $4,800, and BC $5,300.

102. *Making Ends Meet, The 2001-2002 Student Financial Survey,* Ekos Research Associates for the Canada Millennium Foundation, 2003.

103. *Who goes to post-secondary education and when: Pathways chosen by 20-year-olds.*

104. A. Jackson and S. Schetagne, *Still Struggling: An Update on Teenagers at Work,* Canadian Council on Social Development, 2001.

105. Nancy Carr, "Industry specific guide to summer jobs – An expert's view," *Montreal Gazette*, April 18, 2002.

106. *Making Ends Meet,* 2003.

107. *Still Struggling: An Update on Teenagers at Work.*

108. *Making Ends Meet.*

109. Caroline Alphonso, "All work, no play—and still struggling," The Globe and Mail, March 27, 2004.

110. "All work, no play—and still struggling."

111. *Making Ends Meet.*

112. *Making Ends Meet.*

113. An exception is Ontario income tax regulations, which allow parents to claim students as dependents for five years after they graduate from high school.

114. Provinces that apply the bursary to reduce a student's loan are Manitoba, New Brunswick, Newfoundland and Labrador, Nova Scotia, P.E.I., and Saskatchewan. Other provinces and territories give a cash award when the student enrols in his or her second term.

115. *Who goes to post-secondary education and when: Pathways chosen by 20-year-olds; Making Ends Meet.*

116. Statistics Canada, *The Daily,* April 26, 2004; R. Finnie, "Borrowing and burden," *Education Quarterly Review,* vol. 8, no. 4, 2002.

117. *The Daily,* April 26, 2004. The loan limit has recently been increased to $210 a week.

118. *The Daily.*

119. Human Resources Development Canada, *Canada Student Loan Program,* 2002.

120. Low-income as measured by education level of parents, in R. Finnie, "Borrowing and burden."

121. R. Finnie, "Borrowing and burden."

122. E. Dianne Looker, *Why Don't They Go On? Factors Affecting the Decisions of Canadian Youth Not to Pursue Post-secondary Education.*

EATING THE WEDDING GIFTS

CHAPTER 9

123. Vern L. Bengston, T.J. Bilarz, and R.E.L. Roberts, *How Families Still Matter, A Longitudinal Study of Youth in Two Generations,* 2002.

124. *How Families Still Matter,* 2002.

125. Human Resources Development Canada, *National Occupational Classification 4143, Educational Counsellors,* 2001.

126. Canadian Career Development Foundation, *Role of Guidance in Post-Secondary Planning,* 2003. Provinces surveyed were Newfoundland, New Brunswick, Manitoba, and Saskatchewan.

127. See Human Resources Development Canada, *National Occupational Classification 4141, Secondary School Teachers,* 2001.

128. Social Planning Council of Hamilton and District, *Project Impact,* 1994.

129. "Dynamic mentoring program is making a difference," *Toronto Star,* March 27, 2003.

130. Alberta Women's Science Network, *Operation Minerva 2003;* Bill Corbett, Mentoring program helps direct women to science, *APEGGA Newsletter, 2002.*

131. Terri MacDonald, "Junior high female role model intervention improves science persistence and attitudes in girls over time," Evaluation report prepared for *Operation Minerva,* undated.

CHAPTER 10

132. J.F. Gentleman and E. Park, "Divorce in the 1990s," *Health Reports,* autumn 1997.

133. Kathleen Gerson, *Hard Choices, How Women Decide about Work, Career, and Motherhood,* 1985.

134. Statistics Canada, *2001 Census.*

Index

EATING THE WEDDING GIFTS